# Communal Problem and Religion in India



Dr. Rakesh Kumar Arya

DIAMOND BOOKS
www.diamondbooks.in

| | | |
|---|---|---|
| **Publisher** | : | **Diamond Pocket Books (P) Ltd.**<br>X-30, Okhla Industrial Area,<br>Phase-II, New Delhi-110020 |
| Phone | : | 011-40712200 |
| E-mail | : | wecare@diamondbooks.in |
| Website | : | www.diamondbooks.in |
| Edition | : | 2026 |
| Printed By | : | Repro (India) |

---

**Communal Problem and Religion in India**

Author - *Dr. Rakesh Kumar Arya*

Translated by - *Shweta Arya*

*(D/o Dr. Rakesh Kumar Arya)*

# Preface

Some people have called religion an "opium." This is because the intoxication of religion prevents a person from becoming human. Religion makes a person- Hindu, Muslim, Christian, Sikh, demon, and many other things, but it does not make them human.

If a person is viewed from a religious perspective, the observer will see them as Hindu, Muslim, Sikh, or Christian. In fact, nowadays, people's thinking has become so narrow that they interact with others only after looking at or asking about their caste and sect. If two or more people begin a conversation, it is often seen that they first inquire about each other's sect and caste. Who is more humanitarian? Who is more humane-minded? Who is more knowledgeable? There is no discussion on this. There is no exchange of any information.

This view of those who view each other based on caste or sect is truly contrary to human dignity. Religion, which creates such a barrier between humans, was declared an "opium" by Western political thinkers, declaring it a personal matter. Although the Western world has not yet overcome caste, sect, and racism, its society is even more complex than India's, and people have to face it. This is because prominent Western scholars are seen to be deeply invested in the idea of bringing the world under the banner of Christianity. The situation with Islam is even worse.

Indeed, even the declaration of calling religion an opium would be considered foolish. Because if a person's personal thoughts and ideas are frenzied, full of passion, and contain feelings of hatred towards each other, it cannot but have an impact on social life. Avoiding jaggery while eating *gulagula* is truly foolish. Unfortunately, the world has adopted this illogical thinking of eating *gulagula* and avoiding jaggery. The result has made humans and humanity victims of numerous contradictions and complexities.

Therefore, the need was not, and is not, to declare religion a personal matter; rather, the need was to humanize human thinking. Unfortunately, this was not achieved. What a wrong concept it is that, despite being human, you should think like a demon and act like a human. If the thinking is demonic, then the actions are bound to be demonic. Because actions are shaped by thoughts or feelings. Western political thinkers and intellectuals made the mistake of believing that thinking is the foundation of our actions. They did not consider human feelings or thoughts. They should have considered that as long as thoughts are impure, actions are bound to be impure. That is why the Vedas commanded humans -

*"Manurbhavah Janaya Daivyam Janam"*

(Meaning, make yourself human and produce divine progeny.)

The Vedas are telling humans that if you must become something, then become human. What does this mean? Isn't man human? If the Vedas were created for humans, then why did they need to say this to humans? If we consider this, we realize that the truth is that the Vedas were created for humans, but despite being human, humans are not human. Humans were born as animals. They don't become human until they find companionship with humans and inculcate humanity within them. This humanity is the religion of humans. When humans act inspired by this humanity, they become the best human beings in the world.

Thus, it becomes clear that religion sustains and sustains humans. It helps shape their lives. Therefore, a human devoid of religion can never truly become human. A true human being is one who speaks of religion, is religious, and believes in living a life in accordance with it. He believes in acting thoughtfully and intentionally, and who begins his work after considering the consequences of his actions. All the sects in the world speak of humanism, are seen speaking of humanity, and mullahs, clerics, priests, and fathers all give lengthy speeches on humanity, yet they fail to act on the above-mentioned instructions of the Vedas, which realize the human creation plan.

No one thinks that we will consider the consequences of work at the very beginning and will only do what is in the best interest of humanity, in the best interest of all human beings and creatures, in accordance with the commandments of the Almighty God, and conducive to the maintenance of the laws of creation.

Today's so-called civilized humanity fights in the name of religion, but is not seen working to make this natural law of religion universal and widespread.

Irfan Hussain writes in his article, '*Demons of the Past*':

"Although historical events must be evaluated in the context of their times, it cannot be denied that even during that bloody period of history, no mercy was shown to the unfortunate Hindus who fell in the path of the Arab conquerors of Sindh and South Punjab or the Central Asians from Afghanistan... The Muslim heroes who are fondly mentioned in our history books committed some terrible crimes. Mahmud Ghazni, Qutbuddin Aibak, Balban, Muhammad bin Qasim, and Sultan Muhammad Tughlaq all have blood on their hands that has not been cleansed even after years... From the Hindu perspective, the Muslim invasion of their homeland was an irreparable disaster."

"Their temples were destroyed, their idols were smashed, their women were raped, their men were killed or enslaved. When Mahmud of Ghazni entered Somnath on one of his annual invasions, he massacred all 50,000 inhabitants. Aibak killed and enslaved millions. The list of horrors is long and painful. These conquerors justified their actions by claiming that it was their religious duty to slaughter non-believers. Wrapping themselves in the banner of Islam, they claimed they were fighting for their religion, when in reality, they were simply engaging in slaughter and plunder..."

**A sample of contemporary eyewitness accounts of invaders and rulers during the Indian conquests**

The Afghan ruler Mahmud al-Ghazni invaded India at least seventeen times between 1001 and 1026 CE. The book *Tarikh-i-Yamini*, written by his secretary, details several episodes of his bloody military campaigns: "The blood of the infidels flowed so profusely [in the Indian city of Thanesar] that, despite its purity, its stream changed colour and people were unable to drink it... The infidels left the fort and tried to cross the foaming river... But many of them were killed, captured or drowned... About fifty thousand people were killed."

Cooperation, tolerance, sensitivity, goodwill, compassion, kindness, forgiveness, mutual love, etc., are all considered human qualities because they are the essential components of human *dharma*. Religions and sects, using the guise of these very human qualities, have deceived and plundered humanity, bringing disgrace upon humanity. If you look at world history, 90% of the wars were caused by these religions and sects. Not only this, even today the world feels terrorized and intimidated by these religious extremist organizations. The sole reason why followers of Christianity set out to plunder the world was to make their religion the world's religion. Its madness had so taken hold of their minds that they considered it the best system in the world.

When Islam opened its eyes, it too prioritized spreading disbelief in the world, so that the world would come under its flag. Islamic terrorism continues to operate on this very same thinking even today. Even today, religious fanaticism is a key driver behind all the terrorist organizations in the world. These religious terrorist organizations seek to set the world on fire and revel in shedding the blood of its people. Fueled by religious fanaticism, people establish and work for terrorist organizations. Furthermore, religious countries also provide these terrorist organizations with some form of protection. Despite this, a phrase has been coined to mislead people: a terrorist has no religion. If a person who works 24 hours a day for religion and, in accordance with its nature, sets society and the world on fire, doesn't belong to a religion, then whose religion does it belong to?

The phrase *"a terrorist has no religion"* has been coined very wisely. Because under the guise of this phrase, the demonic nature of religion remains protected, and the lie that religion does not teach mutual enmity continues to circulate in society. Islamic terrorists want the entire world to be Islamized, that no non-Muslim should remain in the world. Everyone should become Muslim.

Where every person's thinking is such that they do not consider those of the opposite faith as human beings and are engaged in plotting to destroy their individuality, it cannot be said that *'religion does not teach mutual enmity.'*

We believe that instead of this, we should say that *'religion itself teaches mutual enmity.'* This book was created with this very idea in mind.

Today is the scientific age. Maintaining environmental balance is becoming increasingly difficult due to human folly.

This is because Islam does not believe in animals having souls. Therefore, slaughtering and eating them has become its religious nature. It's not that there are no non-vegetarians among Hindus. Contrary to Vedic religion, people here have also adopted the inhumane practice of killing and eating animals, contributing significantly to the environmental imbalance. According to one estimate, humans, known as the sons of the earth, have wiped out 75,000 species of animals from this earth. Why did this happen?

Considering this, we realize that even in this scientific age, people who believe in rationalism, still make fun of God and divine power. The advancement of materialistic science has spread atheism in the world. This is because the progress of materialism increases human ego. Currently, spiritual progress in the world is almost nonexistent. Spiritual progress makes a person egoless, and theism grows strongly within them. Those pursuing materialistic progress are influenced by religious beliefs, on the basis of which they are creating a world that reflects their thoughts and beliefs. This is natural. Because if their home is built on such beliefs, then the world will also be built on similar beliefs. We must keep in mind that a home creates a world, but the world never creates a home.

How foolish is this notion that even where millions of people adhere to the same religious belief, they are expected to keep this belief private. In reality, this cannot be true. Their religious tradition has become a law, having gained acceptance among millions.

The sacrifice offered by Muslims on Bakrid is an example of this tradition. Tell me, which law in this world has succeeded in keeping this belief private? Religious beliefs are based on the faith and belief of millions of people, which any government thinks about not once but a hundred times before changing or amending them. Therefore, this sacrifice costs the lives of millions of animals every year. You cannot keep this belief private. Therefore, those who say that religious beliefs should be adopted at the personal level, they too are merely spreading a web of words.

In India, Hindus consider the cow sacred, while Muslims consider sacrificing it superior. Consequently, this religious belief often becomes a source of tension between the two communities. Religious fanaticism is the source of this tension. If Muslims rise above religion and consider the importance of environmental balance and the cow's usefulness, the cow is as sacred to them as it is to Hindus, yet they are not seen practicing it.

An article by Mufti Khalil Ahmed Qasmi, Imam of the Jama Masjid in Noida Sector 8, published in Dainik Jagran on February 2, 2004, reinforces this belief. In the article, he considers the sacrifice of sheep, goats, cows, bulls, buffaloes, buffaloes, and camels as *halal*, meaning appropriate. Now, when these people declare cow sacrifice appropriate, while Hindus declare it illegitimate, what will be the consequences? You know very well. Therefore, governments should intervene at their own level. Strict laws should be enacted, and strict action should be taken against those found disturbing the ecological balance or seeking to plunge the world into tension or terror based on personal religious beliefs.

If you ask the above-mentioned Imam whether lions, cheetahs, etc. are halal or not, the Imam covers his ears in remorse. The only reason for this is that even if someone were to kill a lion, cheetah, or other animals, the cheetah and lion are certain to slaughter the killer. It turns out that these people talk about killing and eating those who are innocent, helpless, and unable to help themselves, which is an even greater sin.

Today, there is a need to refine religious beliefs. We need to see how much benefit religious beliefs are providing to the world, society, humanity, and all living beings. Those who still prioritize religious beliefs solely because they believe it will hurt the sentiments of a particular community, and who derive pleasure from such hurt sentiments, should understand that they have not learned anything from that cruel period of history that saw countless wars waged on the basis of religion, shedding rivers of blood. What was the result of such wars, besides harming humanity? What is the point of saying that humanity should learn from history and understand that continuing to embrace things that have proven meaningless in the past is a grave mistake.

In today's scientific age, we should leave meaningless things behind and focus on meaningful considerations and work to establish human values that benefit humanity.

Destroying God's creations in His name is not religious. Those who destroy God's creations in His name are actually atheists, communals, but not religious (*Dharmik*) at all. One who does not love God's creation, that is, creation, and the things God has created, cannot truly be called a devotee of God. Today, the need is to remove the intoxication of religious opium and instill the intoxication of humanity. Only this will make the creation of a civilized society possible. Replacing fanaticism with love and hatred with compassion is the need of the hour.

It is the duty of all religious leaders, religious scholars, clerics, priests, pundits, and conscious citizens of society to contribute to creating a new environment in society by interpreting the beliefs of their respective religions in a humane and humane manner. Only this will make the creation of a grand India possible. To make India a world leader, we must resolve to promote India's humane culture and cultivate a humanitarian approach, abandoning our personal interests.

**-Author**

# Author's note

Dear readers!

I actually published this book in 2004-05 as a small booklet. Ever since, I had been thinking about expanding this topic. The book gained immense popularity at the time. Many people printed and distributed thousands of copies, which made me realize the immense need for this topic. Now, I have attempted to bring this topic to you in detail through this book.

This book was originally written in Hindi. My primary interest is promoting the Hindi language, but due to significant readers' demand, it is now being published in English as well. My daughter, Shweta Arya, has made a significant contribution.

We have not written this book against any particular class or community. An effort has been made to present the truth as it is. Our sole objective is to correct mistakes and improve the present by learning from history to build a better society.

I especially thank Shri Narender Kumar Verma, Chairman of Diamond Pocket Books, for publishing the book and for his pious work in bringing it to readers as quickly as possible.

Finally, I also thank the Almighty God, whose infinite grace has enabled me to undertake this sacred task of writing this book. My family and I are deeply indebted to His grace. I am also deeply indebted to my revered parents, the late Mrs. Satyavati Arya and Mr. Rajendra Singh Arya, my elder brothers, Professor Vijendra Singh Arya, Major Veer Singh Arya, and Mr. Devendra Singh Arya,

Advocate, my wife, Mrs. Richa Arya, and my family, loved ones, friends, and discerning readers, whose blessings and loving support have kept this work going.

I hope this book, like my other books, will also enhance your enjoyment and I will certainly receive your blessings.

Sincerely,

**Dr. Rakesh Kumar Arya**
Mob.: 9911169917

*Address: Dayanand Street, Satyaraj Bhavan*
*(near Maharishi Dayanand Vatika),*
*CE-121, Ansal Golf Links 2,*
*Tilpata Chowk, Greater Noida,*
*Gautam Budh Nagar (U.P.)-201306*

# Contents

*Chapter 1*

# Religious Opium Ruins the Country

Some have labeled religion an "opium." Although those who say so have expressed their opinion by considering religion a synonym or a synonym for religion, the truth is that there is a world of difference between religion and faith. Religion is truly an opium, an intoxicant that prevents humans from remaining human and, turning them into devils, forces them to commit every despicable act unimaginable. World history is replete with such despicable acts committed by humans, causing immense harm to humanity.

"Religious Opium Ruins the Country.
Humanity is Silent, the Sound of Devilism Remains."
*(mazahabi apheem se hua desh barbaad.*
*manavata hui maun hai daanavata ka naad.)*

Religion Brings Destruction, Remember This.

Religion, a Symbol of Development, Teaches the Lessons of Humanity.

*(mazahab laye vinaash ko baat baandh lo gaanth.*
*dharm prateek vikas ka de maanavata ka paath..)*

This religion makes a person a Hindu, a Muslim, a Sikh, a Christian, but never a human being. Whereas religion, instead of making a person religious, makes them religious and shows them the path from human to deity. This is why, while religion wreaks havoc on destruction, religion, by bringing the cool breeze of development, creates humanity. Those who view humanity from a religious perspective see Hindus, Muslims, Sikhs, and Christians in them. This viewpoint is actually contrary to human dignity. There is joy in seeing and understanding each other as human beings. Because such a perspective reflects broadness. Their narrow-mindedness vanishes, and they can observe their human society from a correct perspective.

"The vision of religion is divine;
The radiance of divine religion is divine."
Humanity becomes dull without religion.

*(dharm ki drshti divy hai divy dharm ka tej.*
*manushyata bin dharm ke ho jaati nistej..)*

## Criminalization of Politics

Religion has oppressed humanity for nearly 2,000 years. Religious terrorism is as old as religious beliefs themselves. This religion, which has oppressed the world for so long, was labeled "opium" by Western thinkers, and later by communist ideology, because it prevents world peace. In fact, it is religious ideology that has allowed atheism to spread throughout the world. By killing religion, religion has caused immense harm to the world. Those who have seen the ghost of religion dancing naked in society and bathing in the blood of countless innocent people have come to believe that religion is a deadly disease, from which it is best to maintain distance. This is why people talk about separating religion and politics. Because religion is murderous, it has also made politics murderous, i.e., criminal. Religion has played a crucial role in criminalizing politics. Consequently, religion has also succeeded in politicizing criminals.

Some people have even described religion as a personal matter. However, we do not consider this belief to be correct, because if a person's personal thinking and thoughts are insane, filled with arrogance, and filled with hatred towards others, then such thinking, thoughts, and emotions cannot but have an impact on social life.

As a result, a society formed by such a mentality will clearly reflect anarchy and intolerance. We must keep in mind that a society filled with anarchy and intolerance can never be called a humane society. In such a situation, India's belief that a person's personal thinking and thoughts should be of the highest and purest order is appropriate. Because only through the purity of a person's personal thinking and thoughts is it possible to establish a pure and ideal society. If in our personal lives we act under the influence of a particular religious narrow-mindedness, the impact of that narrow-mindedness will be equally visible in both our personality and actions. The result will be that we will continue to carry our religious narrow-mindedness with us in society, leading to anarchy.

"Corrupted thinking corrupts all societies.
Kingdoms are destroyed by drowning in disease and sorrow."

*(Dushit chintan se bane dushit sarv samaaj.
Rog-shok mein doobakar mit jaate hain raaj.)*

"Abandon lowliness and embrace religion.
Adopt a sense of duty, it will take you beyond the cycle of life."

*(Tyag deejie neechata dharm karo sveekaar,
kartavy-bhaav apanaiye karega bhav se paar.)*

In such a situation, we clearly believe that there was no need to declare religion a private matter, but rather to humanize human thinking. However, religious believers did not allow such a notion to take hold. The result was that society began to be governed by individual thinking. All the dictators and extremist sultans and kings in the world have attempted to forcibly impose their personal views of a particular religion on society and all the people of the world, leading to the spread of anarchy and extremism throughout the world.

It is a very unfair, illogical, and unscientific notion to allow a person to maintain extremist and demonic thinking while expecting them to perform humane actions. This is somewhat akin to keeping today's youth away from the teachings of celibacy, but expecting them to refrain from doing anything immoral or inappropriate that would hamper the honor of sisters and daughters in society.

In his famous poem, *"Saare Jahan Se Achchha Hindustan Hamara,"* Iqbal wrote:

> "Religion does not teach us to harbor enmity among ourselves.
> We are Hindus, we are our country, Hindustan is ours."
>
> *"Mazahab nahin sikhaata, aapas mein vair rakhana.*
> *Hindi hain, ham vatan hain, hindostaan hamaara.."*

The Congress attempted to give this Urdu poem of patriotism by poet Allama Iqbal even greater prominence than Bankim Chandra Chatterjee's *"Vande Mataram."* The Congress did so solely because of its disastrous policy of Muslim appeasement. It should be noted that this same Iqbal had joined Jinnah in the name of breaking up the country. When he was leaving India with Jinnah, he did not even once remember that the Hindustan he was leaving behind was better than the whole world. He left behind Hindustan, which has now become a land of terror. He was so deeply influenced by religion that he forgot his faith in India. He even forgot the oath or pledge he had submitted to Mother India after singing- *"Saare Jahan Se Achchha Hindustan Hamara."* This single example alone reveals how dangerous religion and religious thinking can be for humanity.

Now, what impact could the song of a person who, blinded by religion, has forgotten his faith in his country have? This can easily be imagined.

## Religion is not a sacred concept

Some people view religion as a sacred concept. It is a highly subtle, emotional insight, belief, and faith. Essentially, in the field of spirituality, religion is a perceptual process based on the mind's faith or belief in God, the Prophet, etc. It transcends external pomp, hostility, superstition, etc.

We believe that calling religion a sacred concept from any perspective is foolish. The sacred concept inherent in the word religion establishes a sacred relationship not only between humans but also with all living creatures, making them protectors of all living beings. Religion, on the other hand, forgets about the salvation of other creatures through humans, but instead makes humans thirsty for the blood of other creatures. Ever since Islam arrived in India, it has considered setting records of bloodshed and massacres its greatest religious duty. Outside India, the sword of Islam has also committed religious massacres. Furthermore, Christianity has massacred a large number of people of opposing faiths to propagate its religion. However, a religious person is far removed from any such thinking that involves genocide or bloodshed.

It is clear that a religious person's entire thinking and attention is spent in negativity or destructive tendencies, while a religious person's entire thinking is spent in positivity or creativity. A religious person indulges in destructive tendencies, while a religious person is engaged in destroying destructive or destructive forces from the world. The former seeks peace in the religious sword, while the latter seeks peace in the winds of non-violence, showers of love, and showers of truth.

"Religion, engrossed in destruction, is hostile to all.
Religion worships love and prays for everyone's well-being."

*(mazahab magn vinash mein karata sab se vair.
dharm pujari hai prem ka maange sabaki khair..)*

"Practice truth, non-violence, and love daily.
Eradicate religious sentiments, for they cause genocide."

*(saty, ahinsa, prem ka karo nity vyaapaar.
majahabi bhaavmitaiye karata narasanhaar..)*

Allama Iqbal, who sang the song- *"Religion does not teach us to bear any grudges,"* witnessed the massacre of thousands of Hindus in the name of religion. Gandhi, Nehru, and other Congressmen, who tried to make this song more acceptable to the people of India by giving it even more prominence than *"Vande Mataram,"* witnessed the beheading of Hindu sisters and daughters. It is a different matter that despite all this, Iqbal's song remained an ideal for Gandhi, Nehru, and their Congress colleagues.

## Many hardships endured for the liberation of Ram Janmabhoomi

There are many people in our country who consider the Mughals to be the epitome of secularism. In saying this, they ignore the fact that the temple of Maryada Purushottam Shri Ramchandra Ji in Ayodhya was razed to the ground in 1528 AD by Babur, the very person who initiated the rule of these same Mughals, solely in the name of religion. From then until 1947, and from 1947 until 2019, how much suffering and sacrifice did Hindus endure to regain the birthplace of the most virtuous Ram? Not a single secular Mughal or Muslim felt moved by those hardships and sacrifices. They continued to sing the praises of the Babri Masjid and agreed with them, demonstrating their religious fanaticism.

If religion truly did not teach hatred, then during the Mughal rule in India after 1528 AD, some Mughal ruler would have certainly considered the idea that if, due to religious fanaticism, the Babri Masjid was built in place of the Shri Ram temple, it should be returned with respect to the Hindu community for the construction of a new temple. But this did not happen, because the germ of religion that entered the minds of the Mughals in 1528 AD remained intact for the remainder of their reign and even after that, remains intact even today. If the Mughals' aim had been to create social harmony in the country, they would not have demonstrated communal thinking, destroyed any Hindu religious site, nor sexually exploited women in the name of religion. They would have adopted a humanitarian approach and declared that humanity is paramount for them, and they accept all the good aspects of Hinduism that encourage humanitarian thinking. Had the Mughals displayed such largesse, surely there would not have been a single rebellion against them by Hindus.

In independent India, the Congress and Communists, who have cultivated an image as the Mughals' adopted sons, have been attempting to establish the Babri Masjid, built on the Ram Janmabhoomi in Ayodhya, as an example of India's secularism. Not only this, the Congress party even questioned the existence of Lord Rama. It is clear that if the Congress party and other secular political parties in India, who share its views, were advocating for the Babri Masjid or questioning the existence of Lord Rama in order to preserve India's secular character, they were doing so solely to appease religion. When politics becomes a matter of religious appeasement, it spreads such germs in society that poison the entire environment.

The religion (*Dharma*) of politics is fair conduct. Mind-bending religion (*Majhab*). leads to a multitude of disasters.

*(Rajaneeti ka dharm hai nyaayasheel vyavahaar.*
*Mati bhang majahab kare anarath kee bharamaar..)*

"Politics has become a prostitute and forgotten the national duty. National policy has been forgotten and the fundamental error has been committed."

*(Rajaneeti veshya banee raashtradharm gae bhool.*
*Rashtraneeti bisara daee kar dee mool mein bhool..)*

Truly, such politics is directionless, fostering ideologies that are harmful to society and the country for its own selfish interests. Such politics fails to provide justice to its citizens and, due to its bias, becomes a burden on society and the country. Such politics, inundating society with mischief, leads to the deterioration of human consciousness. The distances seen in India today, based on social and religious differences, are the result of such directionless politics. This is the fundamental mistake of Indian democracy and Indian politicians.

## The Double-Faced Politics of Politicians

It is a very interesting fact about India that while people repeatedly repeat the above line of Allama Iqbal, saying, *"Religion does not teach us to bear enmity among ourselves,"* they are also heard advocating that religion should be kept away from politics. Now, if religion does not teach us to bear enmity among ourselves, then why is there talk of keeping religion away from politics? If religion is so sacred and so conducive to social harmony, then what's the harm in integrating it with politics? If religion can impart such teachings to politics that inspire us to refrain from mutual hostility, what's the harm in that? We should keep in mind that those who advocate for keeping religion away from politics only issue such statements when a leader who speaks of Hindutva speaks of implementing the ideal principles of Hindutva in politics, on the basis of which humanism can be nurtured. What this means is that if Hindutva is discussed, they feel the need to separate politics and religion, and if appeasement of Islam is discussed, they find an opportunity to utter the refrain, *"Religion does not teach us to harbor mutual hostility."*

"Communal narrow-mindedness is the root of religion. Country and religion go to hell, it spreads thorns."

*(Sampradaayik sankeernata hai majahab ka mool.*
*Desh-dharm jaen bhaad mein bikharaata hai shool..)*

We should also keep in mind that if a Muslim slaughters a cow or bull on a festival, it's less a matter of celebrating the festival and more a desire to tease Hindus. In fact, this feeling of teasing Hindus stems from religious narrow-mindedness. Politics fuels this narrow-mindedness of Muslims and displays its own inferiority by allowing them to slaughter cows or bulls.

Indeed, after independence, politics in India has considered itself inferior to religion. Moreover, at times, it has even danced to the tune of religion. When Salman Rushdie boldly wrote about the reality of Islam, politics couldn't muster the courage to say that what he wrote was correct.

When Muslims began issuing decrees against Salman Rushdie, politics chose to hide its face even then. At that time, politics should have stepped forward to break down the narrow walls of religion or attack religious orthodoxy. In the Shah Bano case, politics appeared to be licking the feet of religion. Those who had been advocating that religion and politics should remain separate, then began advocating that religion and politics should unite to attack Shah Bano. Politics, too, proved completely shameless. Standing on the shoulders of religion, it attacked a helpless woman, and through that one helpless woman, ruthless politics killed countless Shah Banos with a single arrow.

Once, the Mahabharata was fought over the disrobing of Draupadi, while the politics of that time possessed both religion and shame. But today's irreligious, secular, and shameless politics itself engaged in disrobing Draupadi.

Those who claimed that religion doesn't teach mutual hostility have now found it clear that half the Muslim world's population has been victimized by male-dominated society's own hatred. Neither politics nor the so-called religious leaders could do anything. Everyone surrendered to religion.

We used to hear that *"whoever has the stick, owns the buffalo (Might is Right)"* but we saw with our own eyes that whoever has religion, politics became his. Religion began to drive the buffalo of politics.

## Religion has divided India

A bird's eye view of India's history reveals that when India, in the form of Aryavarta, had expanded to the Aryans, i.e., Iran, it was religion that initiated the process of carving off its fragments, i.e., provinces, into separate countries. This same religious virus first separated the Aryan (Iranian) province from India, then, in due course, separated Afghanistan, and then, in due course, separated Pakistan.

Not only this, to conceal this horrific nature of religion, some historians emerged in the name of religion. They erased all traces of this murder of history by religion. They wrote history so cleanly that the ghost of religion was suppressed and its misdeeds were also covered up. This is also a prime example of religion harboring enmity towards India. While people may say that religion does not teach hatred, we would certainly say that religion teaches hatred not only against individuals but also against entire countries. That is why it has even tampered with India's history to vent its hatred.

Some people believe that India's partition was due to the fanaticism of a handful of people, but in reality, their assertion only reflects their traditional thinking and policy of Muslim appeasement. The truth is that the majority of Muslims favor dividing the country. This is evident in the fact that when the National Assembly elections were held in 1945, 93% of the country's Muslims supported the Muslim League, making it clear that they favored dividing the country.

It is clear that this feeling of dividing the country, that is, demanding a country within the country, was instilled within them by religion. After independence, the tendency to drive out Hindus from Muslim-majority areas in the country also arose due to this religious thinking.

We witnessed the exodus of Hindus from Kashmir in 1989-90. Just a few days ago, a news report about Mewat in Haryana revealed that Muslims have selectively driven out Hindus from most villages there or converted them from Hindu to Muslim, rendering those villages Hindu-free.

In fact, religious leaders and religious leaders, who incite people against each other through hate speech, play a significant role in fostering feelings of hostility. Undoubtedly, this work is mostly carried out by those who profess Islam.

Today, the need is for people to forget religious thinking, religious education, and religious ideology and welcome good ideas that serve the national interest. By adopting them, they demonstrate their participation and usefulness in the nation-building project.

❒

*Chapter 2*

# Quran's Teachings to Infidels

No matter how much Gandhiji said:

"God Allah, your name is God, may God grant you all sammati."

*"Eeshvar allaah tero naam sabako sammati de bhagavaan."*

This song had no impact on Muslim communalism.

It continued to pursue its agenda. This kind of chanting by Gandhiji certainly confused those who considered themselves Gandhians. Inspired by Gandhiji and encouraged by Gandhism, these people tried shouting the slogan- *"Hindus and Muslims are brothers",* thousands of times across the country, but this slogan failed to unite them. The reason is that somewhere in the fundamental thinking of Muslims, there is a distortion that prevents them from becoming brothers.

Somewhere in the fundamental thinking of Muslims, if possible, investigate. If you can remove the fault, you will gain true understanding. The country suffers from religious thinking. The fear-reliever brothers become terrorists and evil people forever.

Allah's command to Muslims is:

"...And the Jews say that Uzair is the son of Allah, and the Christians say that Christ is the son of Allah. These are their words. They have started making up stories like those of the infidels who came before them (Hindus, Buddhists, and Jains). May Allah destroy them, where are they going astray? (*Surah Tauba 9, Para 10, Verse 30*)"

This provision of the Quran constitutes a significant interference with God's creation. According to it, all people in the world, from the beginning of creation or before Islam, have been astray because of their infidelity, and Islam's purpose is to destroy them. For this reason, a prayer is offered here, that Allah destroy them. This prayer is not like the Vedas, that those who are lost in ignorance and illiteracy should attain true knowledge and improve their lives, and that we should all help the ignorant and uneducated people progress in their lives. In fact, it is this very thought of the Quran that prevents Muslims from coming close to Hindus.

How should those who do not believe in the Quran be treated? This is also clarified in the Quran.

- As for the polytheists with whom you (Muslims) made a covenant (peace), Allah and His Prophet have given them the answer: -

(*Surah Tauba 9, Para 10, Verse 1*)

So travel around the country for four months (*Ziqad, Dhul Hijjah, Muharram, and Rajab*), and know that you will not be able to defeat Allah, and Allah humiliates the disbelievers. And on the day of *Hajj Akbar* (the great pilgrimage), a proclamation is made to the people on behalf of Allah and His Prophet that Allah and His Prophet are different from the polytheists (Hindus, Sikhs, Jews, Christians, Buddhists, Jains)....

This ruling clearly shows that for Muslims, not only Hindus are infidels, but those who follow every religion or sect in the world are infidels, and their aim is to destroy them.

Yes. That is, Allah and His Prophet are only and only Muslims.

- But if you repent (i.e. become Muslims), it is good for you. But if you turn away (from the religion of Islam), then know that you will not be able to defeat Allah. And give the good news of a painful punishment to the infidels (i.e. for terrorizing and causing chaos among the people of the world through any kind of terrorist act).

"Then when the months of Adab (*Ziqad, Dhul-Hijjah, Muharram, and Rajab*) have passed, kill the polytheists wherever you find them, arrest them, surround them, and lie in wait for them at every place of ambush. Then if they repent, establish prayer, and pay *Zakat*, then leave their path (for then they will become Muslims). Indeed, Allah is Forgiving, Most Merciful..."

These are the verses that Wasim Rizvi is asking the court to remove from the Quran.

## The Quran Made Man the Enemy of Man

These teachings of the Quran have turned man into man's enemy. Instead of bridging the gaps between each other, they have attempted to widen or deepen the gaps on the basis of sectarianism. The tendency in the world to attack by ambush or take someone's life by deceit has developed from such teachings of Islam. Prior to this, in India's Vedic tradition, even in war, using weapons against an unarmed person, ambushing someone, or taking someone's life by deceit was considered a crime. However, to serve one's own selfish interests, the Quran completely absolved every individual of these crimes, declaring that they could pursue their own ends as they saw fit.

This is the result of this: today, in the world, humans are stooping to the lowest level of crime to achieve their own ends. Such teachings certainly cannot be considered religious teachings. The people of the country should support Rizvi Sahib's voice.

These teachings clearly demonstrate the virus within religion that creates divisions between sects and prevents members of one sect, i.e. Muslims, from coexisting with members of another sect, i.e. infidels. With such inhumane teachings, how can anyone believe that a Muslim can coexist with infidels?

No matter how much human beings may express hatred towards one another in their behavior, their inner selves have been searching for love since time immemorial. The inner hunger is to find love, to surrender to the Supreme Father and attain that infinite and blissful peace, after attaining which, man has nothing left to attain. He desires to quench the raging fire within, so that he can see love pouring everywhere. He desires to bathe in the blissful rain of love, bringing all the world's human beings under its gentle showers and making them useful to other creatures. The Vedas offer similar humanistic teachings, which the Quran completely rejects.

Humans' inner desire is to manifest harmony, kindness, friendship, and compassion towards one another. However, their external actions are meant to ignite the fire and increase hatred. Unfortunately, the Quran, instead of furthering this human quest for inner discovery, began to fuel external tendencies that set the world on fire. Religion, of course, fuels this fire-fueling and hatred.

## Allah's Islam and Mullah's Islam

Many Muslim intellectuals advocate distinguishing between Allah's Islam and Mullah's Islam. They argue that Allah's Islam teaches brotherhood, while Mullah's Islam teaches setting the world on fire. Whatever the truth may be, it is important to understand that when Islam was in its infancy, it was taken over by some so-called political figures who, in the name of promoting Islam, entered politics engaging in hooliganism and began the process of annexing countries in the name of Islam.

This was a very appealing idea to the Caliphs, or leaders, of Islam. They saw that some political thugs had begun to advance to clear the ground for them, whose ultimate benefit would be the expansion of Islam.

Considering this, they quickly struck a deal with these political thugs. Through the cooperation or close proximity of these political thugs and fundamentalists of Islam, both politics and religion became one. In unison, they embarked on the path of destroying the "infidels" from the world. We don't know whether Islam was politicized or whether Islam politicized criminals to serve its own interests. But whatever happened was not in the best interests of humanity. This began the process that, over the next hundreds of years, led to the slaughter or enslavement of millions of people worldwide, subjecting them to inhumane torture. They looted their wealth, plundered their women, and perpetrated massive massacres in the name of Islam.

After this, a secret agreement was reached between Allah's Islam and the Mullah's Islam, those among these thugs who became kings, sultans, or generals wrote a history of massacres across the world that is solely a history of religious fanaticism, religious hysteria, and fanatic communalism, in which the corpses of humanity are strewn everywhere. If we examine this religiously frenzied history of Islam, we will also find the bodies of millions of people scattered across the Indian pages of Islamic history.

These people, through their cruelty, ruthlessness, inhumanity, and brutality, conquered the noble powers of the world. When they wrote the history of their so-called victory, they labeled that noble power foolish, infidel, ignorant, and who knows what else, and buried it in the dustbin of history as if it never existed, or if it did exist, its existence in the world posed a grave threat to Allah's creation.

This kind of behavior by these people was the gravest crime against humanity. Unfortunately, the people who wrote history have established this crime as a virtue, and we are reading it that way.

These people made all the noble men of the world believe that now that they have begun the process of building the world according to the Quranic message, the world is being bound together by brotherhood and peace. In reality, this kind of campaign by those who believe in the Quran was a campaign to murder humanity. This was understood by the Vedic believers of India from day one. This was why they resolved to oppose Islam from day one. Because they realized that if this inhuman culture spread throughout the world, it would lead to the destruction of the entire world.

## The Relationship between Islam and Terrorism

Can any scholar, historian, or writer tell us the total number of people killed in these massacres when these believers, using the Quran's message as a pretext, were spreading terror and massacring people? Can it also be said whether Islamic terrorism is a thing of the past, tomorrow, or the day before, or was it linked to terrorism from its inception? Scholars like Tariq Fatah and Mahendrapal Arya, the former Imam of a royal mosque in Baraut, say that terrorism and Islam are interdependent. Islam cannot be imagined without terrorism, nor can terrorism be imagined without Islam. This terrorism, spread in the name of religion, began killing people from day one and stained world history with blood. This is its greatest achievement.

This trend of Islam has continued from day one to today. Arsh Danish writes in *'The Wire'* on February 15, 2015:

"According to the 2016 Global Terrorism Index, ISIS, Boko Haram, the Taliban, and al-Qaeda were responsible for 74 percent of deaths from terrorism.

All these organizations foster religious extremist ideas. Because of the religious dimension of current terrorism, a large section of scholars is trying to understand how Islamic terrorist organizations use religion to create a narrative that attracts vulnerable individuals."

In fact, we should not believe the sweet words of brotherhood that so-called Islamic scholars appear to us on TV channels or in articles they publish in newspapers and magazines, but rather understand the "truth of Islam." TV channel owners should also invite to debates only those Islamic figures who have the courage to accept the truth of Islam and are capable of giving the world such a noble thought that can spread humanity and spread peace and love everywhere.

According to a news item published in *'Patrika'* on December 9, 2015,

"On the last day of the Urs-e-Rizvi at the Ala Hazrat Dargah in Bareilly, more than 70,000 Muslim religious leaders from around the world issued fatwas against the terrorist organizations ISIS, Taliban, and Al Qaeda. Islamic scholars and religious leaders stated that the views of these organizations are un-Islamic and inhuman.

Their activities are against the fundamental principles of Islam. Such people are not true Muslims. Nearly 1.5 million people participated in the Urs and signed pamphlets against terrorism."

The Muslim scholars in Bareilly who signed and issued this fatwa are truly commendable. Islamic intellectuals should show such courage.

In an article titled *"Islam and Terrorism: Reality vs. Myth,"* written on March 23, 2019, Dr. Mohammad Arif writes,

"We must remember that there is no connection between religion and violence, whether it is Islam or any other religion. Religions came into existence to establish justice and peace in the world, not to seek revenge and spread violence. Retaliation and violence can never be a part of any religion. And in Islam, the question of that does not even arise. Islam does not support terrorism but condemns it.

According to Nahida, just as people carry out various professions, spreading terror and violence is the profession of terrorists. They have nothing to do with any religion and should be considered only savage beasts, certainly not the flag-bearers of any religion."

The word Islam is derived from the root '*salam*', which means peace. In essence, the word '*salam*' is the essence of Islam. It means establishing peace and submitting to the will of Allah. Islam does not even indirectly advocate oppression, let alone violence. The conditions accepted by the Prophet Muhammad in the Treaty of Hudaibiyah were not in favor of Muslims, but to avoid violence, he accepted the conditions that established peace.

Islam does not, in principle, condone the use of violence. If conflict ever arises, *the Quran, verse 2:90*, clearly commands:

"Fight in the way of Allah against those who fight against you, but do not be aggressive. Allah certainly does not like aggressors. Here, fighting in the way of Allah means fighting for justice, for the establishment of a kind and compassionate society, not for violence."

We do not agree with all of Arif Sahib's points above, but we would certainly like to say that when Islam's political heirs, leaders, or caliphs, were conspiring to destroy humanity by misinterpreting Islam, at that very moment, Islam's so-called pacifist nature and its humanitarian thinking were essentially auctioned off.

It is also worth noting that if Islam was truly a pacifist religion, there should have been a tradition of people who believed in it as a "peaceful religion," which is nowhere to be seen today.

If Islam was truly founded to establish peace, and the true meaning of Islam is precisely what Arif Sahib is saying, then Islamic scholars of all time should have made it a point to ensure that no one would shed blood or persecute followers of any other religion in the name of Islam. But certainly, no meaningful initiatives or efforts were made in this direction by Islamic scholars and political leaders. This is the cause of greatest concern.

Ram Yadav, author of *'The Dangerous Cloud of Terrorism Over Europe,'* writes,

"Leaders, religious figures, and most intellectuals in the Islamic world have been reluctant to unequivocally condemn Islamist terrorist groups and their terrorist attacks, issue fatwas, socially boycott them, or punish the terrorists.

They have been washing their hands off the issue by claiming, 'Terrorism has no connection to Islam,' or 'Terrorists have no religion.' The public has grown weary of hearing this rhetoric. The suspicion is beginning to grow stronger that the Islamic world is secretly in solidarity with the terrorists and perhaps believes that by seeking to Islamize the world, they are following the dictates of the Quran. While some introspection has certainly entered the Islamic world's thinking, it is not sufficient to accommodate Western sensibilities." (From *"Web Duniya"*)

Ram Yadav's concern is entirely justified. People talk for superficial appearances. They don't strongly condemn what is happening on the ground, nor are they seen opposing those who commit such evil acts. On the contrary, they are seen supporting or defending those who spread terrorism in the name of Islam.

These people know that everything their people are doing in the name of Islamic terrorism is in accordance with the commandments of their holy book. Therefore, while they may say such things to gain praise among the Hindu community, in reality, they are in agreement with the members of their own community, because they know that Allah has clearly commanded them not to spare the infidels at any cost.

Such systems have attempted to convince Muslims that their God is also a Muslim. When such communal prejudice takes root in people even towards the Supreme Being, the Creator of the universe, it gives rise to radical communalism.

❐

## Chapter 3

# Religion Swallows Civilizations

Islam divides the world into the "party of Allah" and the "party of Satan." This is also known as "Dar al-Islam" and "Dar al-Harb." In fact, it is this fundamental thinking that prevents Islam from harmonizing with other religions. Islam views followers of other religions with a discriminatory viewpoint. Because of this discriminatory viewpoint, Islam does not even recognize the fundamental rights of followers of other religions. This is why the question of fundamental rights for followers of other religions in any Islamic country remains as serious today as it was at the time of Islam's birth. The unfortunate situation is that Islam is not even willing to break away from this thinking. Many Muslim writers and scholars are trying to bring Islam out of this perspective, but their efforts are proving unsuccessful. This is because the majority of people who support fanaticism in Islam are in the majority.

While a large group of Islamic interpreters, calling Islam a religion of brotherhood and peace, insist that those who harbor hatred for Islam have neglected to reveal its true nature and that Islam has never had such a concept as Darul Harb or Darul Islam, within Islam itself, Islamic scholars like Maulana Maududi, founder of Jamaat-e-Islami, strongly advocate the principles of Darul Islam and Darul Harb.

Even from the perspective of these scholars, Islam and its scholars are either dismissive or hostile toward those who are not in the party of Allah or toward countries that have yet to be Islamized. Their *jihad* will continue until the entire world is imbued with Islam. What I mean to say is that these people, directly or indirectly, appear to advocate genocide and bloodshed until the entire world accepts Islam or joins the party of Allah.

Communists and other similar ideologues consider Islam and Christianity to be symbols of progress. Islam, on the other hand, will continue to destroy anyone who holds a different ideology until that person is completely destroyed and the entire world is subjugated to a single ideology. In reality, this tendency of Islam violates people's freedom of speech and expression. It does not allow people the freedom to develop spiritually, mentally, and physically, but instead seeks to confine them within limits and bind them to the stake of a single narrow ideology.

Until the entire world is immersed in Islam, until the Quran prevails throughout the world, this cycle of massacres will continue, and this world will burn in the fire of barbarity.

With this kind of attitude and thinking, all other religions in the world must either abandon their identity and convert to Islam or be prepared to die. Overall, this cycle of *jihad*, terrorism, and hatred based on religion is unstoppable.

The tradition of issuing fatwas in Islam is enough to reject the judiciary of any country. Muslims accept the judicial system or state system of any country only as long as their numbers are very small. As long as Muslims are in very small numbers, they demonstrate complete loyalty to the judicial system and state system of any country, demonstrating that there is no better person than themselves. As their numbers grow, their demands also increase. Gradually, a time comes when, after reaching a sufficient number, they begin to challenge the constitution, the judicial system, and the state system of that country. They declare:

"We love only our law. We accept nothing else except Him. We consider the Quran to be divine revelation and the Sharia to be the most unique law in the world."

"This is why, as soon as Muslims become a majority in any country, they Islamize it by changing its constitution and other constitutional provisions. If we examine the history of those countries around the world that have today declared themselves "Islamic States," it becomes clear that this same process was adopted to Islamize them.

Had Gandhiji studied and understood this aspect of Islam, he would have been able to grasp the Islamic perspective in the context of India. It seems that Gandhiji either did not understand this aspect of Islam, or even after understanding it, he remained ignorant, holding himself and his Congress party, after him, Hindu fundamentalists, responsible for the partition of the country. Gandhiji's Muslim appeasement has been extremely harmful for our country. It cannot be said that Gandhiji was unaware of the fundamental nature of Islam. The truth is that despite understanding its fundamental nature, Gandhiji pretended not to understand it. This pretense forced the country to pay a heavy price. It was he who emphasized the fact that "*Religion does not teach us to hate each other*." This idea of his was further promoted by the country's first Prime Minister, Pandit Jawaharlal Nehru.

By singing the line, "*Religion does not teach us to hate each other*," an attempt has been made to cover up all the atrocities and sins committed against India, which have led to its current disintegration.

Historical scholars believe that there once existed a degenerate branch of Brahmins in India, known as Shaikhs. This degenerate branch of Indian Brahmins still resides in Iran and Arabia, known to us as Shaikhs. The country of Arabia is derived from the Sanskrit word "*Arva*," which means horse or stable. Therefore, Arabistan means a place where high-quality horses are found. Arabian horses are still famous in our country. Forgetting our own language, we have done ourselves a great disservice by imitating the languages of other countries. If we had continued to love and respect our own language, there are many words that could have taken us on a journey through history. "*Arva*" is one of them.

In fact, it was India's Sanskrit language that gave rise to the names of geographical locations across the globe. These words originated from the Sanskrit language. Over time, these Sanskrit names were corrupted and transformed into names of local dialects, depending on the country, time, and circumstances. This led us to believe that these names were derived from these languages. We believe that all the languages in the world, apart from Sanskrit, are dialects, which people named to glorify them.

The entire Arab region was governed and disciplined by India's Vedic culture. However, when idol worship became prevalent in Vedic culture due to Jains and Buddhists, Muhammad led a revolution against it, leading to the emergence of Islam on the land of Arabia.

From the perspective of a social reformer, blowing the trumpet of revolution against the previous system can be considered a very good quality of Muhammad's personality. Later, the way he himself or his successors began massacring the "infidels" and launched a campaign to convert the entire Arab region, which believed in Vedic culture, to Islam through the Islamic Revolution cannot be justified from any perspective. It would have been better if he had explained his principles to the people with love and affection and inspired them to navigate the world from a Vedic perspective.

Those who chant, "*Religion does not teach us to bear enmity among ourselves*," do not know that the entire Arab region was the land of the Aryans, which religion swallowed and snatched from the Aryans and handed over to Islam, or rather, by converting the Aryans and infusing them with its own image, handed over to Islam. Iran, too, was the land of the Aryans, but religion replaced it with Islam instead of Aryans. Some Vedic scholars believe that the word "Arab" originated from the name of the sage Arva, the grandfather of Parashurama. Some scholars believe that today's The province of Parsia is also named after Parashurama. Whatever the case, juxtaposing such words with Indian legends clearly demonstrates that the Aryan religion of India once reigned supreme in all these provinces.

This glorious history of India's Vedic culture has been slain by this demon called religion. Historians and writers who harbor hatred for India have deliberately consigned it to obscurity, preventing India's current young generation from understanding its past. It should also be clear that the global expansion of Indian cultural nationalism has been constrained by the demon called religion.

## Characteristics of Muslims

Scholars have a clear assessment of whether Muslims are loyal to any country they live in. Their characteristic is that, as long as they constitute 2% of the population in a country, they strive to portray themselves as peaceful, tolerant, law-abiding, civilized, and well-educated individuals. At that time, they portray themselves as 'peacemakers.' This 'peacemaker' image attracts others, or rather, deceives them. This deception proves fatal for them. Over time, some people are drawn to Islam through deception, while others are drawn to Islam through pressure.

For example, in the United States, Australia, Canada, China, Italy, and Norway, the Muslim population currently ranges from 0.6% to 2%, yet here they present themselves as highly tolerant and constitutionally abiding citizens.

It is also a notorious fact about Muslims that when their numbers reach between 2% and 5%, they begin to "preach" to their followers. Through this preaching, they target lower-class members of other communities. They attempt to increase their numbers by converting them to their own community, thus distorting the demographic statistics of that country or place. This assimilation of poor people into their community is also essential for them because they want to rapidly change their population. Denmark, Germany, Britain, Spain, and Thailand are countries where the Muslim population still remains below 5%. Due to the small Muslim population here, Islamic terrorism has not yet manifested in its most serious form. However, the governments here have also understood this type of trickery played by Muslims. This is why the US is exercising extreme caution even with the activities of a handful of Muslims. It does not want to take any risk that could harm its country's future.

Targeting the poor sections of any country or society and increasing its numbers is one of the fundamental principles of Islam, through which it gradually establishes its control over a country. Poor people can be easily deceived by offering them money, etc., and Islamists take advantage of this.

As soon as they exceed 5% of the population, Muslims begin to exert their influence on the governments and social organizations of the respective countries. They then form social organizations and try to pressure the governments through protests or other such measures, which leads to governments succumbing to their pressure.

In many Western countries, they forced governments and organizations to allow halal meat. Among these countries,

France, the Philippines, Sweden, Switzerland, the Netherlands, and Trinidad & Tobago are particularly noteworthy.

As soon as Muslims exceed 10% of the population, they begin to talk about implementing their Sharia law in the respective region or country. They then begin to smell the foul smell of that country's constitution, constitutional decorum, and constitutional rules, and begin working on the plan that it would be best if the country's major constitutions, rules, and regulations were changed and adapted to Sharia law. To carry out this thinking and plan, they gradually begin to consider the laws of the respective region or country as obstacles and, by demanding that their own personal laws be implemented there, they create law and order situations for the governments. To this end, they also resort to tactics like vandalism, protests, and demonstrations. The riots in France, the cartoon controversy in Denmark, and the vehicle attacks in Amsterdam are all examples of this kind of Muslim thinking.

As soon as the Muslim population exceeds 20%, *Jihadi* talk begins in the respective region or country. Religious intolerance and killings begin, so that people can be motivated to convert to Islam by instilling fear and terror. The reason such incidents are increasing day by day in India is that the number of Muslims here has now reached the threshold required for *Jihad*.

When the population exceeds 40%, a large number of mass killings and terrorist activities are carried out. Countries like Bosnia, Chad, and Lebanon, where the Muslim population has exceeded 40%, are currently experiencing such incidents in significant numbers. When the Muslim population reaches 60% in any region or country, a mass 'cleansing campaign' of people from other communities or groups is launched. This is what happened in Kashmir, India.

We, the people of India, should take special note of the events unfolding in Kashmir. We must keep in mind that what happened in Kashmir in 1989-90 was a well-planned scheme to Islamize Kashmir. To date, no Muslim leader from any party has responded to this situation in a way that could strengthen nationalism or resettle Hindus who fled the Kashmir Valley. No Muslim leader is talking about re-settling the Hindus expelled from Kashmir. Islam attacked Kashmir's Hindus, the Pandits, before our very eyes, and Kashmir was rendered devoid of Hindus. Yet, we continue to live under the illusion that one day all Kashmiri Pandits will be resettled in Kashmir.

In Albania, Malaysia, Qatar, Sudan, etc., the Muslim population has exceeded 60%, where such incidents occur daily. As soon as the population surpasses 80%, large-scale cleansing is carried out, with clear government patronage. Thus, Muslims consider it their fundamental right to snatch or violate the fundamental rights of the 20% of people from other communities.

It should be noted that this is happening in the same country where, when Muslims themselves comprised less than 20% of the population, they were fully enjoying their fundamental rights. However, when other communities became 20% in the same country, taking away their fundamental rights became the fundamental right of Muslims. Then, there is no one in that country to speak out or even listen to the rights of any minority community. Meaning, the entire country becomes a prison for such a minority population. Upon reaching such a stage, any country rapidly progresses towards becoming 100% Muslim. Then, very soon, we see that the country has become completely Muslim. Praise-makers of Islam, historians, and writers then proudly write that this country, influenced by the brotherhood of Islam, has become "Islamized," thus giving rise to another Islamic nation in the world.

Working on this very plan, many countries now have a Muslim population of more than 80%. Prominent among these are Bangladesh (83%), Egypt (90%), Gaza Strip (98%), Iran (98%), Iraq (97%), Jordan (93%), Morocco (98%), Pakistan (97%), Syria (90%), United Arab Emirates (96%) while Afghanistan, Saudi Arabia, Somalia, Yemen are such countries where the entire population has accepted Islam.

(You can find all these statistics in detail in Dr. Peter Hammond's book - *'Slavery, Terrorism and Islam - The Historical Roots and Contemporary Threat'* and Leon Uris - *'The Hajj'*.)

This entire game of going from zero to one hundred is played out as part of a well-planned conspiracy. Behind it stands the demon called religion. This demon is carefully concealed. To conceal it, words like brotherhood, peace, and harmony are repeatedly used, and countries are lured by them. By the time people's eyes open, they realize that much destruction has already occurred.

India's secular leaders need to understand this destructive plan of Islam to understand this entire game of religion. Today, those whose eyes are open are not only seeing much of the past but also seeing much about India's future. There is still time for the people of the country to break away from the foolish notion that 'religion does not teach hatred among people' and understand that it is religion that teaches people to hate each other.

Religion itself is the enemy; religion itself is the murderer, the robber of justice, destroying the destination of peace. Ignorance is the one who searches for flowers of peace here, setting the garden on fire, and is not worthy of respect.

It is also worth understanding that even in countries that are 100% Islamized, peace, brotherhood, and harmony are not established. Even there, their so-called urn of peace breaks, and when it does, it is revealed that it was filled not with nectar but with the poison of hatred. The result is that people then engage in fighting, quarreling, and killing each other on ethnic grounds.

Those who have been forcibly converted to Islam are filled with resentment and anger against those who forced them to do so. Those who forcibly converted to Islam are filled with the feeling that they are inferior to us, that they were formerly Hindus, and therefore it is not right to associate them with them. People have the mentality that they have been our slaves in the past and are still our slaves today. This racial hatred thus becomes the cause of discord and conflict among them. Only by understanding this kind of conspiracy and mentality of the people of Islam, we realize that it is religion that swallows civilizations.

Even after achieving a 100% Islamic population, people still experience the same sorrow, suffering, pain, regret, crime, violence, etc. Then we realize that the peace we sought has become even more distant from us. The inner confusion increases so much that a person finds himself trapped in a prison where the more he struggles to get out, the more he feels trapped in its tortures.

It is the job of religion to create further entanglement. Religion's job is to protect us from ignorance, narrow-mindedness, hypocrisy, and true misguidance, and to further entangle us in this misguidance. Religion further strengthens the human weaknesses of ignorance, narrow-mindedness, hypocrisy, and oppression, and increases the tendency towards bloodshed in the world. Whereas, religion aims to calm these troubles and, by teaching the lesson of humanity, elevate humanity above all humankind, transforming it into a divine and majestic being. Islam is far from this spirit of religion.

Certainly, pseudo-secular leaders, intellectuals, and Muslim scholars should consider how to rescue the world from this pitiable situation. Without indulging in any communal thinking, these people should accept this truth and make serious efforts to save the world from it. All decisions, all thoughts, and all ideas should be based on humanism. Wherever religious individuals are working to incite violence and hatred among people on the basis of religion, they should be handed over to the law for engaging in anti-social, anti-national, and anti-human activities. Whereas, those who, by embracing humanitarian thinking, are engaged in eliminating discrimination and distance between humans should be encouraged as well-wishers of humanity.

❐

*Chapter 4*

# Islamic Invasion and Hindu Oppression

Oppression and religion are inextricably linked. Wherever there is religious thinking, there is inevitably oppression of those of the opposite faith. Oppression reveals the extremist nature of religion. As for Islam, every ruler who followed it, from the very first day of their reign, spared no effort in persecuting infidels, heretics, or those of the opposite faith. It would not be an exaggeration to say that Islam persecuted followers of other religions to its fullest extent. It crossed all limits of cruelty.

A look at the history of India reveals that from the day people were introduced to Islam, the dark pages of extremism and oppression began to be associated with India's history. The people of India had many experiences that they witnessed firsthand in the form of Islamic invasions and the atrocities committed by them. Such incidents as rape of women, looting, and massacres, were unknown to the people of India before the Islamic invasion.

Upon coming into contact with India, the Islamic invaders forcibly converted countless people to Islam and committed inhuman atrocities against them, committing ruthless massacres that make the pen shudder at the mere mention of them. These atrocities committed by the Islamic rulers have either been omitted from Indian history or have been greatly minimized by so-called scholars and historians. Although there have been many impartial Muslim scholars who have accurately depicted and provided unbiased information about the communal atrocities and riots that occurred during the reign of their respective rulers, the accounts provided by such Muslim scholars have been deliberately suppressed.

## Educational centers destroyed

Religious places destroyed. Many such magnificent temples of learning were destroyed. During the reign of these communal Islamic rulers, numerous Hindu religious places were destroyed. Many magnificent temples of learning were destroyed, once renowned as centers of learning for the entire world. The entire world benefited from these educational centers. Numerous scientific discoveries were made through these educational centers, universities, and gurukuls. The destruction of these centers of knowledge and science was a grave disservice to humanity. The destruction of these centers of knowledge and science was not merely the collapse of a few brick walls; rather, their collapse was a deterioration of humanity, and should have been documented in history. Historians have simply considered the collapse of a few brick walls. This casts doubt on the impartiality of such historians.

In India, mentioning knowledge and science is considered an essential part of history. However, current history does not even consider it appropriate to lament the destruction of centers of knowledge and science. This clearly shows that this history was written by sycophantic historians, subservient to politicians.

Speech has become silent on cruelty and crime. Silence has fallen on sin. Who will tell the truth?

## The Hindu Past of Countries

Muslim rulers, notorious for their religious discrimination and oppression, enslaved Hindus and sold them for a pittance in the markets. It's impossible to even describe the various ways in which many people were enslaved and transported to their own countries, as if they never existed.

It's a notorious historical fact that not only present-day Pakistan but also Afghanistan, Iran, Iraq, and many Arab countries, which were originally Vedic, were converted to Islam.

Even though countries like Pakistan, Afghanistan, and Malaysia have now become completely Islamic, their ancestors endured similar atrocities at the hands of Islam. It's because of these atrocities that Islam's flag is still flying high there today. All of these countries have a Hindu past. They either don't know about it now or remain silent about it even after knowing it. Even the people of India are taught such history that they cannot become familiar with the Hindu past of these countries.

How unfortunate is it that these people of Pakistan, Afghanistan, and Malaysia can neither call the sacrifices of their ancestors at that time as sacrifice nor can they praise their pledge to preserve their religion? These poor people only know that 'ignorant people' lived here at that time and that Islam began spreading its 'brotherhood' here by killing them. Despite knowing this, they hesitate to call those so-called 'ignorant people' their ancestors. It is understandable that the people of these countries call or consider their ancestors ignorant, but it is difficult to understand that the people of India should also call the Pakistanis of that time ignorant. Because the ancestors of all these countries, including Pakistan, were the descendants of Ram and Krishna. Even if they were reminded today that their ancestors were Shri Ram and Shri Krishna, they would not be willing to accept it. They are troubled not only by India's political glory but also by its cultural pride.

Viewed from this perspective, religion first disconnects a person from their glorious history, from their ancestors, and from the chain that has connected them to a clan and lineage since the beginning of creation. Influenced by this very characteristic of religion, Indian Muslims hesitate to call themselves descendants of Ram and Krishna. They even maintain a distance from it despite knowing that their ancestors were once Hindus.

## Muhammad bin Qasim's Invasion and Hindus

Although Arab invasions of India began as early as 638 AD, the most prominent invader was Muhammad bin Qasim, who arrived in India in 712 AD and fought with the then Hindu king of Sindh, Dahir. King Dahir fought tooth and nail to protect his country's culture and religion. After the war, Muhammad bin Qasim committed numerous atrocities. The only reason for this was that he had invaded India with the imperialist ideology of Islam. The primary purpose of his sword was to spread Islam and destroy heretics.

Inspired by this very purpose of his sword, Muhammad bin Qasim destroyed numerous Hindu temples and shattered numerous idols in an attempt to punish "infidel" Hindus. His approach was entirely Hindu annihilation, which is often downplayed by calling it politically motivated. He forcibly converted many people to Islam, and many Indians were enslaved and deported to Iraq. A large number of Hindus were massacred. He unleashed terror in India in 712 AD.

One of the objectives of this invasion led by Muhammad bin Qasim was the plunder of Indian temples. At that time, a temple on the seashore in Karachi was covered in a large amount of gold, which Arab traders could see from afar. The reflection of the temple's gold in the water became a source of immense greed for them. Inspired by this, Arab traders posed as invaders, forming a gang of robbers and bandits, and invaded India.

In Indian history, the British are taught as traders and robbers, but in reality, the facts about these Islamic robbers are not clarified: on what basis did they come to India as robbers and continue to plunder here for so long?

Islamic robbers, rapists, criminals, and bandits are described as ideal rulers of our country, as if they possessed all human qualities. If these people had faith in temples and humanity had found a place in their thoughts, they would never have attacked India under the influence of communal views.

## Invasions of Mahmud Ghaznavi

Mahmud Ghaznavi was a major Islamic invader who invaded India after Muhammad bin Qasim. He, too, was influenced by the Islamic religious perspective. His primary objective was the plundering of temples and the spread of Islam in India. He also contributed to the traditional narrative of Islamic terrorism, which is highly appreciated within Islam.

This was the same foreign invader who attacked India's famous Somnath Temple in 1026 AD. Although India, under the leadership of the Gurjar ruler Bhimdev, succeeded in driving away this foreign invader. The Somnath Temple, a symbol of India's cultural identity, was repeatedly destroyed by foreign Muslim invaders thereafter. Their actions were motivated by communal hatred.

We should also note that Mahmud Ghaznavi succeeded in destroying the Somnath Temple only after the sacrifice of 50,000 Indian warriors. At that time, Gurjareshwar Bhimdev was also fighting against the invader and was seriously injured on the battlefield. Only after his injury was Mahmud Ghaznavi able to carry out his heinous act of temple destruction. When King Bhimdev regained consciousness, he contacted the kings of other states like Jalore and Ajmer and, describing the destruction of the Somnath temple as a matter of national identity, requested the rulers of those states to jointly confront this foreign invader. By doing so, the king not only attempted to shake the pride of those kings but also proved his own patriotism and nationalism.

The king stirred the valor of his fellow kings and reminded them how they were descendants of mighty warriors like Bhima. Many kings were descendants of emperors and emperors who had contributed to the glory of India.

It was a good thing that all the kingdoms from which King Bhimdev had requested military assistance accepted his request. By then, Mahmud Ghaznavi was also living in the areas around Somnath, committing massacres, plunder, and other diabolical atrocities. King Bhimdev was finding it increasingly difficult for this monster to remain in India. He did not want this wolf to remain in India and further distress the indigenous people.

The kings who provided military assistance to King Bhimdev also saw this serious question of national identity as a matter of their own prestige and provided him with military assistance as soon as possible. This indicates a sense of nationalism within them. They did not want to leave King Bhimdev alone. When they saw that the nation was facing a crisis, they did not consider themselves untouched by it. Their four-pronged armies decided to confront the foreign invader.

All these facts have been mentioned by Mr. K.M. Munshi in his book "*Imperial Gurjars.*" From him, we learn that when Mahmud Ghaznavi was returning to his country after plundering and massacre in India, a large Gurjar army attacked and wiped out most of his army. This act of resistance by the people of India against the foreign invader was a highly nationalistic act. This resistance by the brave Indian warriors led to the capture of many of Ghaznavi's Turkish warriors, who later converted to Hinduism and settled here. King Bhimdev and his companions avenged their defeat against Mahmud Ghaznavi with great secrecy and strategic skill. It is unfortunate that history recounts his victories, but nothing is written about Bhimdev and his fellow kings who defeated him.

This proves how biased Indian history has been written.

When Mahmud Ghaznavi began his invasions of northwest India in the 11th century, his attacks were aimed at destroying Hindu religious sites, desecrating idols, and Islamizing India. In addition to the famous Somnath temple, this foreign Islamic invader also extensively destroyed temples in Mathura, Thanesar, and Ujjain. According to his court historian, *Al-Utbi*, his invasions of India were part of a "*jihad*" (war) to spread Islam and against non-Islamic practices.

It is noteworthy that when Muslims embark on a "*jihad*," their sole objective is to leave no "infidel" untouched.

Another infamous historical fact about him is that, influenced by Islam's radical religious ideology and anti-Hindu sentiment, he enslaved 5,000 Hindus in Mathura alone. How many people must have sacrificed their lives to save these enslaved Hindu family and loved ones, and how massive a communal riot must have ensued in this situation? There is no mention of this anywhere. It seems to have been deliberately suppressed to create the impression that Hindus never retaliated against Islamic atrocities or to establish the false notion that Islam peacefully Islamized the people of India.

Similar riots must have occurred in protest against every massacre perpetrated by Islamic invaders or rulers and the subsequent enslavement markets established, which were also symbols of Hindu retaliation, but they too have been ignored in history.

Those who claim that every Islamic invader in India propagated Islam, the religion of peace, through peace and never harbored any communal views towards Hindus should understand that, according to strategic historian Victoria Schofield,

"Mahmud Gujnavi's father vowed to liberate the Kabul Valley and Gandhara from Hindus, a pledge his successors upheld. Until 980 AD, the Gandhara region was ruled by Hindu Shahi kings, whose last king, Jaipal, was defeated by Subuktagin."

It is indeed true that Islam and peace are incompatible. Violence and bloodshed are rampant. Raping women is no exception.

## The Truth of the Hindukush Mountains

In what we know today as the Hindukush Mountains, many Hindus had to sacrifice their lives at the hands of Islam's communal sword. Confirming this, historian Ibn Battuta wrote,

"The name of the Hindu Kush Mountains is derived from the many Hindus who died in these mountains, exposed to the cold winds and snow, while being transported from India to Arab countries as bonded slaves."

Mahmud Ghaznavi seemed determined to rid this region of the Hindu Kush of Hindus. He suppressed them to the maximum extent possible with the naked sword of Islam. This is why, according to contemporary historian Alberuni,

"Mahmud so devastated this region that all Hindus left it and went to Kashmir, Varanasi, and other places beyond our reach."

This example demonstrates that Hindus have been forced to leave their homeland many times, just as we were forced to leave the Kashmir Valley before our very eyes.

In 1989, the Marxist government of West Bengal issued an order mandating that the atrocities committed by Muslim rulers against Hindus and the destruction of their temples not be mentioned in history.

In a resolute defense of Muslim atrocities, renowned leftist historian Professor Romila Thapar even wrote that Mahmud Ghaznavi never attacked Somnath. This means that if we find any mention of Mahmud Ghaznavi's attack on Somnath by contemporary writers or historians, it is either fictitious or merely a fabrication of the 'saffron-clad writers' of that time. We are also pleased that Romila Thapar at least admits that the Somnath temple existed at that time; otherwise, one might expect her to claim that the Somnath temple did not exist at the time Mahmud Ghaznavi visited.

From the invasion of Muhammad bin Qasim to the invasion of Ghaznavi, millions of Hindus in our country either suffered their heads at the hands of Islam's communal sword, converted to Islam, or abandoned their settled homes and wandered the forests, earning their living. Thus, the country was plunged into extreme chaos at that time. Behind all this chaos was the intoxication of a communal or religious monster.

In his book, "*Sultan Mahmud of Ghazni*," Professor Muhammad Habib of Aligarh Muslim University writes:

"Mahmud Ghaznavi (Mahmud Ghaznavi) invaded India driven by greed for wealth and power. ... The Sultan's life clearly demonstrates that, whatever his role, he was by no means the ideal embodiment of virtue as fanatic Muslims have portrayed him. His moral character was similar to that of later rulers, neither good nor bad. He was like them in wine, in bartenders, and in battle."

Alberuni writes:

"Mahmud destroyed the country's progress. Like grandmother's tales, he performed such miracles that the Hindus were crushed to pieces and scattered everywhere like dust particles. Their scattered pieces have given rise to a tendency of hatred towards Muslims that will never end."

In fact, only by establishing such facts in Indian history should one examine the character of cruel foreign invaders like Mahmud Ghaznavi. It would be appropriate to let history speak its language.

## Invasions of Muhammad Ghori

Mohammad Ghori launched numerous invasions of India. While he was repeatedly invading India, motivated by the goal of expanding Islam in India and establishing his empire by any means necessary to destroy Hindus, his brother Ghiyasuddin was the ruler of his own country, Ghor. He greatly expanded the Ghori Empire across the Indian subcontinent. To achieve this objective, he launched his first invasion of India in 1175 AD against Multan. Subsequently, Muhammad Ghori launched a second invasion in 1178 AD against Bhima II, the ruler of Patan (Gujarat), in which he was severely defeated.

At the time of Muhammad Ghori's invasion of India, Prithviraj Chauhan's kingdom, established in Delhi and Ajmer, was the dominant power in India. Muhammad Ghori knew well that unless Prithviraj Chauhan was defeated, he would not see his dream of establishing his empire in India come true. Consequently, the first battle between Muhammad Ghori and Prithviraj Chauhan took place in 1191 AD, known as the First Battle of Tarain. Prithviraj Chauhan was victorious in this battle. Driven by his religious beliefs, he too committed arbitrary atrocities against Hindus.

However, in the Second Battle of Tarain, also fought in 1192, Muhammad Ghori succeeded in defeating Prithviraj Chauhan. In both these battles, and in all the other wars he fought in India, the same tactics of temple destruction, forced conversion of Hindus, enslavement, or genocide were played out under his leadership, as were those played out during the times of earlier Islamic invaders.

Not only this, in 1194 AD, Ghori attacked Jaichand's kingdom, Kannauj, and wreaked havoc there, just as he had done when attacking other Hindu kings. In other words, he spared Jaichand and his kingdom, who had helped him. The only reason behind this was that he did so when he needed to seek the help of a non-believer against another non-believer. However, once he had eliminated one non-believer, eliminating another also became his religious objective. In other words, religion inspired him to eliminate Jaichand, and his brotherhood, armed with a drawn sword, set out to slay Jaichand.

❐

*Chapter 5*

# Oppression of Hindus during the Religious Sultanate Period

After numerous attempts to invade India for over 500 years, Islam succeeded in establishing its rule over parts of India in 1206 AD under the name of the Slave Dynasty. It is also a coincidence that Islam, which preaches fraternity, had its first dynasty in India named the Slave Dynasty or the Dasa Dynasty. It is not known whether it was a slave itself or wanted to enslave someone, but whatever it was, it makes it clear that the word 'slave' eliminates any possibility of 'brotherhood.' This clearly conveys the existence of both the ruler and the exploited in such a system. This clearly indicates the existence of both the ruler and the exploited. This suggests that exploitation, oppression, and tyranny are inevitable in such a system. The people of this dynasty were themselves slaves and were preparing to enslave others. Those who were slaves themselves were preparing to enslave others. Even after this, these people have been glorified and presented as ideal rulers.

The very name 'Slave Dynasty' exposes the false notion of Islam's brotherhood: Islam's objective was not to eradicate slavery from the world, but rather to oppress independent nations by propagating the concept of slavery. In any case, there is no connection between brotherhood and slavery.

Those who considered themselves slaves to the Muslim Turk rulers and even felt an attraction to the word "slave" were, in fact, people completely devoid of self-respect. Their sense of self-respect was destroyed by the cruel Muslim Turk rulers. The Aryan Hindu race does not believe in trading anyone's self-respect. Although slaves are found in the saint tradition within Hindu society, they too are not in keeping with the Aryan tradition of Indian knowledge and science. This slave tradition also developed in India at a time when the clouds of ignorance, illiteracy, and hypocrisy were thick everywhere. We have a tradition of Aryan sons yearning for liberation.

After the death of Muhammad Ghori, in 1206 AD, his slave, Qutb ud-Din Aibak, laid the foundation of foreign rule in India for the first time. This new dynasty he established is known in history as the Slave Dynasty.

According to the account of Muslim historian Maulana Hakim Syed Abdul Haji, during Aibak's rule, Hindu, Jain, and Buddhist places of worship were destroyed as part of a religious fanaticism. The remains of 20 Hindu and Jain temples were used in the construction of Quwwat al-Islam, Delhi's first mosque. The remains of ancient temples can still be seen around Qutub Minar, which makes it clear that the Qutub Minar was built after the demolition of ancient temples.

Such work carried out during the time of Qutb ud-Din Aibak is now unraveling many mysteries of history, revealing that Delhi's Qutub Minar has also been misattributed to Qutb ud-Din Aibak. This is why people are now approaching the courts to determine the authenticity of Qutub Minar.

## The Beliefs of Leftist Historians

Leftist historians have consistently defended the communal policies of Muslim rulers. Such historians argue that the Turkish invaders' intention in invading India was not to kill Hindus, seize their property, or commit any kind of atrocity against them. If we examine these Muslim invaders from the perspective of these leftist historians, they seem to be providing evidence to these foreign invaders, claiming that they came to India with a purely humanitarian outlook and to share knowledge. Despite this, if Hindus opposed these invaders, the fault lies with the Hindus because they did not want to accept their superior knowledge.

Leftist historians try to tell us that these invaders came with the vision of making India modern and progressive. The people of India should have welcomed such ideas of these invaders. It was the foolishness of the people of India that they did not want to embrace modernity and progress.

Leftist historians believe that if some Hindus were killed during such invasions, it was only because the king who fought these foreign Turkish invaders was a Hindu, and whose army was naturally composed of Hindus. This logic by leftist historians makes the atrocities of the Turks appear unjust. Furthermore, mention of the massacres of Hindus committed by them has been completely erased. Such facts have been misrepresented in history or the literature of that time, and presented as if the Turkish invaders did not intend to destroy Hindus, which is false.

The country's first Education Minister, Maulana Abul Kalam Azad, encouraged this work of leftist historians to erase Hindu history. In the 19th century, Maulana Abul Kalam Azad himself and other Education Ministers who followed him continued to uphold the beliefs of leftist historians.

**Was it decided from the outset how Hindus should be treated?**

It is clear from the accounts of Ziauddin Barani and Dr. K.A. Nizam that the question of how to treat idol-worshipping Hindus in an Islamic state arose early in the establishment of the Delhi Sultanate. In this context, it is crucial to mention the advisory committee of Muslim scholars formed during the reign of the first ruler of the Delhi Sultanate, Mustafa (peace be upon him), whose advice and guidance the Sultan relied on. This committee's clear view of the political and political perspectives regarding Hindus was that Hindus were the greatest enemies of the Prophet (peace be upon him). This committee clearly indicated and advised the Sultan that treating Hindus with implacable hostility would be the best way to respect the Prophet's sentiments and his holy book.

It goes without saying that Hindus are infidels, and the extermination of infidels is the purpose of the Prophet and his holy book. Therefore, they should be treated with the utmost cruelty. The more they are oppressed, the more the sentiments of the Prophet and the holy book will be respected. It is clear that when actions are motivated by such sentiments, the existence of human virtues like justice, truth, and non-violence is unimaginable.

This committee advised the Sultan that, in order to respect the Prophet's sentiments, it was necessary for him to confiscate Hindu property, violate the chastity of their women, abduct them, and use them as he pleased. Furthermore, humiliating and harassing Hindus was essential for power politics to achieve this sacred objective. (*Ziauddin Barani - Sahifa-e-Naate Mohammadi, pp. 390-91*) This single statement exposes the claim of leftist historians that the Ottoman rulers brought a message of brotherhood to India.

The committee further states that - "Whenever all the various regions and towns of India are filled with Muslims and a large Muslim army is formed, then our order will be to massacre Hindus and force them to accept Islam."

Based on this type of advice, religion continued to control power and politics, and under its leadership, Hindus continued to suffer the cycle of oppression and oppression. This anti-Hindu thinking and policies of Muslim adherents are often completely ignored in history writing.

Sultan Qutb ud-Din Aibak, a slave of Ghori, glorified Islam in India. Purushottam Yoga, author of '*Muslim Political Thought and Aspirations*', tells us on the basis of evidence that Qutb ud-Din Aibak also left no stone unturned in glorifying Islam in India. According to Hasan Nizami:

"After suppressing a rebellion in Kol (Aligarh) in 1193, he erected three minarets of Hindu heads. In 1194, he demolished 27 Jain temples in Delhi. From their rubble, he built the Quwwat-ul-Islam Mosque, which still stands today.

In 1196, after conquering Ramkaran in Gujarat, Aibak put 50,000 infidels to the sword. 20,000 slaves and countless animals fell into the hands of the victor. The city was destroyed and temples were demolished. In 1202, Kalinjar was attacked. Here too, temples were demolished and mosques were built in their place. 50,000 Hindus were put to the gallows of slavery."

Around this time, a 'gentleman' named Muhammad bin Bakhtiyar Khilji was roaming eastern India to establish the dominance of Islam. In 1200, they attacked Bihar's highly unprotected university, Udantipuri, and massacred the Buddhist monks living in the monastery. In 1202, they suddenly attacked Nadia.

According to Badayuni:

"Immense wealth and riches fell into the hands of the Muslims. Bakhtiyar Khilji demolished places of worship and idol temples and replaced them with mosques and khanqahs."

During the Sultanate period, anti-Hindu rulers rose to the pinnacle of power and politics, and during their reigns, they organized numerous celebrations of Hindu genocide. Speaking of the Khilji dynasty, religious leaders and religious rulers, through their generals, continued to massacre large numbers of Hindus during this period. During the Khilji period, Alauddin Khilji's empire was more extensive than that of all the Turkic and Mughal emperors and sultans, so it is natural that the mass massacre of Hindus occurred at a much faster and more widespread scale.

## Atrocities during the reign of Alauddin Khilji

Jalaluddin, Firoz Shah, and Alauddin Khilji's army chiefs, such as Ulugh Khan, Nusrat Khan, Khusrau Khan, and Malik Kafur, launched numerous campaigns in which Hindus were eliminated through mass massacres or organized programs designed to humiliate and degrade them. Looking at these misdeeds, it becomes clear that their minds were filled with only anti-Hindu sentiment. This anti-Hindu sentiment was solely due to their own religious beliefs. Everything they did was driven by the hateful ideology of religion. They made it clear through their conduct that if they harbored any tyrannical feelings toward Hindus, it was solely due to their religious beliefs.

When we read the historically famous incident of Rani Padmini and Alauddin, we should not limit ourselves to just one Rani Padmini and one Alauddin Khilji. Instead, we should understand that when the ruler himself was so adulterous and corrupt in character, how corrupt and degraded in conduct must his generals, army officers, other government officials, and employees have been? When Hindus were insulted by the behavior and actions of such corrupt and degraded people, they would undoubtedly have become aggressive and fought for their honor. Few historians have dared to call this type of Hindu resistance in medieval history. We believe that where such incidents of Hindu resistance occurred, Muslim rulers spared no effort to suppress it. Such conflicts often resulted in Hindu resistance spreading to the streets and neighborhoods, erupting into communal riots, which were then ruthlessly suppressed with government protection.

We must understand that at that time, there were many Alauddin Khiljis who were oppressing Hindu women, and there were many Queen Padminis who either took up swords or committed *Jauhar* to protect their honor. Overall, the identity of Hindu women was violated on a large scale at that time, and their freedom was taken away in the name of religion. Purushottam Yoga himself tells us in his aforementioned book that- "according to Amir Khusro, this Sultan had 30,000 Hindus massacred during the attack on Chittor. Furthermore, there are numerous other allegations against him that indicate that he was extremely harsh towards Hindus."

## Rebellion Raising the Hindu Mind

When we hear and read from Khilji's historians that Hindus revolted in various parts of the Sultanate, such as Punjab, Gujarat, Madhya Pradesh, and Uttar Pradesh, their statement implies that the Hindu public revolted against the religious tactics and distorted forms of power and politics at that time. It is an ancient Indian tradition that if power becomes anti-people, the people have the full right to oppose it.

At that time, there was no democracy; instead, religious bandits ruled the country. Therefore, when the people of India revolted against the government and politics, acting as religious bandits, with their democratic demands, their rebellion was brutally crushed by the bandits in power.

These atrocities often led to mass massacres of all children and adults above the age of eight. Today's Congress and leftist historians either ignore such brutal atrocities or, if they do, present them in a manner that seems as if they were not motivated by communal hatred on the part of the ruling class of that time, but rather were necessary in light of the harassment being inflicted on the ruling class by the country's Hindu community.

The accounts of historians Elliot and Dawson reveal that Alauddin Khilji's commander, Nusrat Khan, imprisoned the women and children of those who participated in this rebellion. He then tortured and humiliated these women in public. Children were slaughtered in front of their mothers. The inhuman practice of abducting wives and children as punishment for men's crimes also originated in our country.

## Alauddin was given advice regarding Hindus

From Elliot and Dowson's book- "History of India" (*Wayback Machine, Vol. 3, Trubner & Co., London, pages 183-185*), we learn that this act of religious violence was orchestrated not only by the army, but also by the Muftis, Qazis, and other courtiers, who gave it religious sanction. Qazi Mughisuddin Bayana advised Alauddin that- "it is lawful to crush and subjugate the Hindus, for they have been the greatest enemies of the Prophet (Muhammad), and, in accordance with the Prophet's command, we must kill, plunder, and imprison them. They must either accept Islam or be killed, enslaved, and their property destroyed."

When Islamic sultans or members of the ruling class issued such orders against Hindus based on their religious scriptures, the entire administrative system or governance apparatus was never able to oppose them, because the entire system of that time had become accustomed to functioning on a communal basis.

Malik Kafur was a very powerful official during Khilji's reign. He was originally a Hindu. He had been forcibly converted. Under his leadership, Khilji's army conducted the first campaign in South India in 1309 AD and the second in

1311 AD. Although he was very generous towards Hindus, it was still very important for him to follow the instructions of his master. This is why, putting aside his generosity, he followed the orders of his emperor, Alauddin Khilji, and during both these military campaigns, he massacred numerous Hindus in South India and destroyed their religious sites.

Historians believe that in addition to the Halebidu temple, many other temples were destroyed. The looted treasure was so vast that 1,000 camels were used to carry it. This loot included the famous Kohinoor diamond, which was set in the eyes of the goddess of the Bhadrakali temple.

Communalism was so rampant that thousands of Hindus lost their lives in no time. Today's leftist and Congress historians, when searching for communalism in India, seem to make illogical attempts to locate it in the 10-20 years before independence. The truth is that the tradition of communal riots and communally motivated massacres began in India the day Islam was introduced to India. Thus, the history of riots in India is as old as the history of the arrival of Islam. Any serious and inquisitive student of history should base his research on this fact while exploring communalism in India.

## The Cycle of Oppression Against Hindus During the Tughlaq Period

The cycle of Islamic communal oppression against Hindus continued unabated even during the rule of the Tughlaq dynasty, which succeeded the Khilji dynasty.

According to Narasimhacharya, Ulugh Khan invaded South India and killed 12,000 unarmed monks in Srirangapatna and destroyed the temple. The Vaishnava philosopher Sri Vedanta Desika hid among the corpses, saving himself and his two sons with the texts written by Sri Sudarshan Suri.

Indeed, this atrocity against the monks is a highly condemnable event in Indian history, as killing unarmed people is considered an act of cowardice, not bravery, in India. If the atrocities of the Islamic invaders are viewed in accordance with this definition of India's heroic tradition, it becomes clear that they never displayed bravery. On the contrary, displaying cruelty and cowardice, they boasted of their bravery by killing unarmed and innocent people. This is considered highly condemnable in Indian historical tradition, but their book tempts these people with the prospect of attaining the position of Ghazi. Driven by this greed, Muslim invaders and rulers committed such heinous crimes against Hindus.

The "*Tarikh-e-Firozshahi*," written during the time of Firoz Shah Tughlaq, provides clear evidence of systematic persecution of Hindus during his reign. At that time, it became fashionable among the ruling class that the more a person, intoxicated with power and position, suppressed, oppressed, and persecuted Hindus, the more heroic and courageous they would be considered. Displaying this false bravery, many Muslim rulers and their generals forcibly converted Hindus, enslaved them, and even destroyed their religious sites.

Firoz Shah's death was a disaster for Hindus. Muslim officials ordered the killing of all Hindu slaves and the destruction of their bodies. This was precisely what happened. The motive behind this was likely that if these slaves were killed along with the emperor, he would receive a high status in heaven, as he would take their souls and offer them to God.

Firoz Shah also persecuted Hindu Brahmins. These were the very people who had refused to accept Islam. The brutality of Islam then created a scene that would move even the most hard-hearted person. This incident is mentioned in the *Tarikh-i-Firoz Shahi*, which states:

"By a decree, a Brahmin was brought before the Sultan. He was told about the true religion (Islam), but he refused to accept it. The infidel was tied hand and foot, thrown onto a pile of wood, and fire was set on both sides. The fire first reached his feet, causing him to scream. Soon, the fire spread all around him." (*Tarikh-i-Firoz Shahi*)

If we consider the harshness of the Tughlaq rule against Hindus, historical texts *(Elliot and Dowson and Munshiram Manoharlal)* reveal that Hindus were forcibly subjected to the Jizya tax, were registered as infidels, and were constantly monitored.

## Islamic terrorism existed even at that time

One reason for the surveillance of Hindus at that time was that Hindus never wholeheartedly accepted foreign Muslim rule. Therefore, they repeatedly rebelled against Muslim oppression, yearning for their independence.

Hindus who installed idols or built temples, or publicly practiced their religion around the pond, were imprisoned and killed in the palace. Such accounts clearly demonstrate that Hindus lived in complete terror at that time, meaning that Islamic terrorism was creating extremely difficult conditions for them even at that time.

## Firoz Shah Tughlaq wrote in his autobiography

"Some Hindus established a shrine in the village of Kohana and began practicing idol worship there. These people were captured and brought before me. I publicly declared this a perverted practice and ordered them executed outside the palace gates. I also ordered all non-Islamic books, idols, and worship materials burned. I subdued the survivors through punishment and threats, so that everyone would know that such non-Islamic practices are forbidden in a Muslim state." *(Firuz Shah Tughlaq, Futuhat-e-Firoz Shahi)*

Many great men in India have, from time to time, launched movements against idol worship. Among them, Maharishi Dayanand is particularly notable. No great man in India has issued a fatwa or order to destroy any idol worshiper in protest against idol worship. On the contrary, people have adopted the path of resolving the misconceptions of idolaters through debate.

❐

## *Chapter 6*

# Timur Lang's Terrorist Campaign

Every invader who organized conquests in the name of Islam, brandished religious fanaticism and extremism, terrorizing the entire world. From this perspective, Islamic terrorism is not a recent phenomenon; it arose with the birth of Islam. It is a different matter that its spread across the globe varied depending on the country, time, and circumstances. One of those Islamic invaders who launched their conquests in the name of Islam was Timur Lang. His own historians say that during his nearly 70-year life, inspired by Islamic terrorism and communal thinking, he launched 35 conquests against India. He wreaked massive destruction in the region from Haridwar to Cairo in the west.

Historians also believe that Timur Lang's resolve to wreak such widespread destruction against India was solely due to his desire to become a Ghazi. Timur himself said,

"I developed a desire to become a Ghazi by leading a campaign against the infidels (Hindus), because I had heard that a Ghazi is one who kills infidels. I couldn't decide whether to go first against the infidels of China or those of India. I took the Quran's command in this regard. The verse I extracted reads:

*'O Prophet! Wage war against the infidels and atheists, and deal with them with extreme severity'.*"

We have taken the above quote from Elliot and Dawson's book. On page 397 of this same book, Timur addressed his people before attacking India, saying, "We may purify and cleanse the land of India from the filth of infidelity by converting the people of that country to Islam, and by destroying their temples and idols, we may be called Ghazis and Mujahids."

According to the Islamic system, there could have been no greater ideal or life purpose for Timur than to come to India to eradicate infidelity (Hinduism) and to use all his might to destroy it. Indeed, the leftists' description of religion as an opium perfectly fits the Islamic invaders, who, intoxicated by the intoxication of religion, led their evil demonic forces towards India and other countries of the world, and considered setting records of plunder, robbery, murder, rape, and genocide as the greatest virtuous act of their time.

In India's knowledge tradition, when a person considers sin to be virtue, it is called human ignorance. This ignorance causes great harm to humanity. An even greater harm occurs when a person considers ignorance to be knowledge and, driven mad by this so-called knowledge, brings immense suffering to the world. This is precisely what Muslims were doing. Their knowledge had gone mad, and they failed to see that the bodies falling to the ground before them were also human beings. In their eyes, they were not human but infidels, and bathing in the blood of infidels had become the greatest reward for them.

Those who suppressed this historical truth by adopting a policy of appeasement have also harmed humanity. Let us assume for a moment that they did this to forget past bitterness and move forward. But those for whom this was done have neither forgotten the bitterness nor moved forward.

They remain bound by the shackles of brutal communalism. They continue to engage in the barbaric acts of fourteen hundred years ago. They have neither forgotten their history nor their historical figures. They are learning from their history and their historical figures and carrying forward their work, and are engaged in their task of bringing the entire world under the banner of Darul Islam.

## When Timur became synonymous with terror

In March 1398, Timur crossed the Indus River near Cuttack, becoming a synonym for terror and destruction for the world. In March 1398, Timur crossed the Indus River near Cuttack and subjected all the Hindus of the town of Tulumb to the brutality of his religious sword, snatching away all their wealth. Thus, in the first blow, thousands of Hindus became scapegoats before Timur's sword. Subsequently, when Timur entered Kashmir, the crown of India, he unleashed a similar havoc there, committing countless ruthless atrocities against Hindus. Thus, he became synonymous with terror.

This cruel foreign invader, driven mad by his religious zeal, even robbed the Hindu farmers of India of their food. His aim was to starve the Indians to death. When he was still not satisfied, he set fire to the plundered areas. Humanity groaned at his atrocities. Shouts and cries of grief could be heard all around. But for Timur, the deaf and mute, these cries became a source of joy rather than sorrow. The reason for his joy was that he had left his home imagining such "enchanting" scenes in his mind.

After establishing his reign of terror in Kashmir, Timur terrorized the infidels with his religious terror in Fatehabad, Rajpur, and Panipat, and finally arrived in Delhi. Many Hindus in Delhi had already learned of Timur's atrocities, including the numerous atrocities he had previously committed in Multan, Dipalpur, Saraswati, Kaithal, and other places. The heartbreaking tales of Timur's atrocities caused many Hindus to flee the capital,

Delhi, or, if they had the opportunity, to escape the invader's brutal atrocities, or to commit suicide or burn their children and wives alive. Those Hindus who survived were subjected to brutality that surpassed all limits. Historians and writers often write a few lines about these heartbreaking incidents of Hindus burning their own children and relatives in self-defense and move on. But when we imagine these horrific scenes or imagine how we would feel if these atrocities were happening to us, we realize how many inhuman and brutal atrocities our ancestors endured to preserve their religion and culture.

## Timur's objective was also the destruction of Hinduism

His biographer, in his book "*Mulfuzat-e-Taimur,*" quotes Timur as saying before departing for Delhi:

"I sent my goods from Tehna. I traveled through forests and mountains. I killed 2,000 devil-like people, captured their wives and children, and plundered all their wealth and cows. The people of Samana, Kaithal, and Aspandi were all heretics, idolaters, infidels, and atheists who set fire to their homes and fled to Delhi with their children, leaving the entire country desolate."

The primary objective of Timur Lang's invasion was to destroy Hinduism. He had a desire to become a Ghazi and an unwavering devotion to religious service. The Ulema and Sufis advised him, "It is the supreme duty of the Sultan who professes Islam and of all those who believe that there is no god but Allah and that Muhammad is the Prophet of Allah, to fight for this purpose, so that their religion may remain safe and their legal system may remain strong, and they may exert themselves to suppress the enemies of their religion. As soon as these joyful words of the learned people reached the ears of the chieftains, their hearts were fixed on waging a religious war in India, and bowing down on their knees, they repeated this chapter of victory." (*Reference: Timur's biography 'Mulfuzat-e-Timur' Elliot and Dowson, Volume III, Page 397*).

Such examples of Islamic invaders reveal that at that time, the Islamic invaders and their armies rushed or galloped toward India like a farmer eagerly heading to his field to harvest his flourishing crop. Indeed, Hindus were like a crop to these Muslim invaders.

## Ten thousand Hindus were slaughtered

At Bhatner, Hindus faced Timur's army. They fought fiercely to defend their religion and freedom, but when victory eluded them, they silently sacrificed their lives on the altar of freedom.

Pages 421-422 of *Timur's biography* state:

"The warriors of Islam attacked the Hindus from all sides and continued fighting until, by the grace of Allah, the efforts of my soldiers saw the ray of victory. In a very short time, all the people in the fort were put to the sword, and ten thousand Hindus were beheaded in a very short period of time. The sword of Islam was thoroughly washed with the blood of the unbelievers, and the entire treasure became the plunder of the soldiers."

Where the ideology of a Muslim hero or role model is such that the earth was washed with the blood of Hindus and Hindu treasures were looted by soldiers, how can it be believed that they believe in the spirit of living in harmony with Hindu society? Those whose role models have despicable ideology, their followers are bound to be despicable as well. Regarding those whom we see today looting Hindu wealth, torturing their sisters and daughters, dreaming of Hindu homes and property becoming theirs after the Islamization of India, or shouting slogans or giving speeches like this, we must understand that all of them are the spiritual sons of Timur Lang. Therefore, it should not be assumed that those who consider Taimur their role model will have a different mindset than Timur.

## Thousands of Hindu women were plundered

The same book further states:

"When I inquired about the Saraswati River, I was told that the people there were ignorant of Islam. I sent my troops in pursuit, and a fierce battle ensued. All the Hindus were slaughtered, their women and children were taken captive, and their possessions and goods became plunder for the Muslims. The soldiers returned with thousands of Hindu women and children. These Hindu women and children were converted to Islam."

The Jats are a Kshatriya caste of India. They have a glorious history. In numerous places, Jat warriors have displayed their bravery and protected the country and religion. The Jats hold an important place among the Kshatriya castes of India. They displayed their valor even during the time of Timur, and gave the enemy a tough fight. Timur has written in his biography :

"It was brought to my notice that these mischievous Jats are as numerous as ants. My great purpose of attacking India was to wage a holy war against the unbelievers. I felt that it was necessary for me to defeat (completely destroy) these Jats. I entered the forests and ravines, and killed two thousand giant Jats. On the same day, a group of Syeds, believers who lived nearby, came to meet me with great humility and courtesy and they were welcomed with great honour. I welcomed their chief with great respect." (*Same book, page 429*)

## One hundred thousand Hindus were massacred

The above biography of Timur states:

"On the twenty-ninth, I advanced again and reached the Yamuna River. On the other bank of the river was the fort of Loni. I decided to conquer Loni immediately. Many Rajputs locked their wives and children in their homes, set them on fire, and then came to the battlefield. They fought like devils (i.e., like valiant warriors) and were ultimately killed. Others in the fort's guard were also fought and killed, while many were taken prisoners. The next day, I ordered that the Muslim prisoners be separated and spared, but that non-Muslims be put to the sword by the converts. I also ordered that the houses of Muslims be kept safe, but all others be looted and destroyed." (*Eliot and Dowson, Volume III, pages 432-33*)

Here, Timur had one hundred thousand Hindus slaughtered in a single day. After the slaughter, he had their severed heads gathered together and mounded. He accomplished this by slaughtering the people of the rural area of Loni. As a result, terror and fear spread far and wide. A foul smell spread everywhere, and the stench took the form of an epidemic. Therefore, many people decided to leave their homes and migrate. Just imagine, how could those Hindus, who immediately consign their dead to the funeral pyre, fearing that their presence would spread the stench, pollute the environment, poison the air, and have a detrimental effect on life and health, endure the stench emanating from one hundred thousand corpses? And how far and wide did the stench of one hundred thousand corpses spread? How terrifying must that scene have been?

Timur Lang begins his biography, "*Tuzuk-e-Timuri*," with this verse from the Quran: "*O Prophet, fight against the infidels and the unbelievers, and be harsh against them.*" He further explains the reason for his invasion of India, writing:

"My goal in invading India is to wage a religious war against the infidel Hindus (described later), so that the army of Islam can also obtain the wealth and valuables of the Hindus."

## Sikandar Butshikan

While Kashmir is a unique example of our Indian cultural heritage, for some time now, Kashmiriyat has been equated with the Ganga-Jamuni culture of Kashmir, in which the Hindus there have been forced to leave. Ever since Islam entered Kashmir, it was as if water caught fire. Voices of unrest began to be heard in the peaceful valley, and blood stains began to appear on the once white sheet of Kashmir.

In the Kashmir Valley, a symbol of peace, sacrifice, austerity, and spiritual practice, Sikandar Shah Miri wrote many bloody tales of Islamic fanaticism.

Reading these stories of ruthlessness and cruelty towards Hindus sends chills down one's spine. This Sikandar Shah Miri, who perpetrated atrocities against Hindus in Kashmir, was called Butshikan because, driven mad by communal frenzy, he committed unprecedented atrocities against Hindus. He destroyed their religious sites and smashed idols wherever he saw them.

It wasn't just Hindus who were persecuted; he also destroyed Buddhist religious sites and forced them to convert to Islam or leave Kashmir. Thus, forcing Hindus to flee Kashmir is not a recent phenomenon; it is a long-standing practice of Muslims. Whenever Islamic atrocities have increased, Hindus have been forced to leave Kashmir.

## Social festivals were also banned

Sikander Shah, demonstrating his communal thinking and policies, also imposed restrictions on the religious and social practices of non-Muslims. He completely banned non-Muslim worship, dancing, singing, music, drinking alcohol, and religious festivals. In this situation, it became extremely difficult for Hindus to live in Kashmir. They faced a life-and-death dilemma. For millions of families who had considered Kashmir their home for years, the only option left was to pack up and flee. In such circumstances, many Hindus, seeking protection from such persecution and atrocities, either converted to Islam or fled Kashmir. Furthermore, some may have felt unsafe in both circumstances and considered suicide the only option. There were also those who were killed in conflicts with Muslims.

When Sikandar Butshikan was destroying Hindu libraries in Kashmir by burning them, patriotic Hindus were not happy with this act. Seeing their cultural heritage destroyed before their eyes, Hindus felt immense pain. Therefore, they also tried to hide their books of knowledge and science by taking them to the caves or inaccessible forests of Himachal.

## Educational centers were also burned to ashes

At that time, Kashmir was a center of learning. Many schools and centers of Vedic education were burned to ashes. Sridhar writes in his *Rajatarangini*:

"Seeing this orgy of destruction of knowledge by the Muslims, the learned men of the time, disguised themselves to save their books, crossed the treacherous mountains, carrying a few books with them, and fled. Thus, for years, these Kashmiri scholars, hiding in the forests and other places, protected India's ancient culture. Even after this, countless rare texts were reduced to ashes in the baths and furnaces of the Sultans."

Kashmir had become a pilgrimage site for those thirsty for the blood of Hindus. Thousands of Syeds came to Kashmir and engaged in the process of converting Indians. These people have been portrayed in history as doing a great favor to Kashmiris by coming to Kashmir, already a center of knowledge and science. Whereas the truth was that through this act, these people were also rendering 'excellent service' to Islam, that is, by helping convert people, they were silently rendering a great service to Islam.

These Syeds came from East and Central Asia. Describing the tragic tale of their atrocities in Srivar Rajatarangini, he writes,

"The story of the Syeds' atrocities is extremely horrific. They crossed the limits of humanity and cruelty. The Syeds killed the physician Pandit Bhuvaneshwar, cut off his sandalwood-coated head and placed it on the highway. To instill fear in the public, the Syeds placed the severed heads among coals and wood on the banks of the Vitasta."

He further writes that- "The bodies of Hindus were thrown into the Vitasta River. They would stink as they floated and drift away into the Mahayadamsar. No one even considered performing their last rites. It was common for women visiting the banks of the Vitasta to be pierced with arrows and their bodies torn apart. Two or three people were impaled daily on the banks of the Vitasta. Beautifully adorned, deriving the exquisite pleasure of touching the grains placed on a cotton cushion, they were seen lying naked on the ground (referring to the aristocratic feudal lords), eating crows, poultry, and wild animals, with worms oozing from their eaten fat and flesh, and stinking. Naked bodies lay like bundles of fuel on the roads from Samudra Math to Purvadhishthana. The officials were murdered without justice, and their bodies were treated cruelly.

From the courtyard of the royal palace to the hips of Chandalas, they (the crown and the petitioner) were dragged with ropes, their body parts were stained with feces. They became food for dogs. When the soldiers were defeated, their heads were cut off and hung on flags."

As far as the use of force is concerned, we learn from '*Masalik ul Ansar*', Elliot and Dowson, Volume III, page 580, about Muhammad bin Tughlaq that- "The Sultan never showed any zeal in his war against non-Muslims (Hindus). The number of Hindu prisoners was so large that several thousand Hindus were sold every day."

Similarly, it is worth noting that- "first of all, those captured during war were given as gifts. After this, the Sultan would gift the daughters of other infidel kings to the rich and important foreigners, and to his own brothers and relatives." (*Reference: India during the Tughlaq period, S.A. Rizvi, Part 1, page 189*).

Ibn Battuta tells us:

"Then the Sultan (Muhammad bin Tughlaq) went on a hunting expedition to Baran, where, under his orders, the entire Hindu country was plundered and destroyed. The Hindu heads were collected and brought back and hung on the walls of the Baran fort."

## Sayyid Dynasty

The reign of the Sayyid dynasty lasted only 37 years. Several rulers of this dynasty ruled from 1414 AD to 1451 AD. Although their reign was brief and they were largely embroiled in internal conflicts, there is no evidence that they showed any kindness towards Hindus, or that the Turkic rulers succeeded in making any radical changes to their traditional Hindu policies. What this means is that the Turkic and Islamic tradition of anti-Hinduism remained intact even during their rule.

## Lodi Dynasty

All the Turkic rulers had no connection to the royal religion. These people, who believed in the religion of plunder, considered plundering India and oppressing its people as their royal religion. In fact, the reign of Islamic rulers in India is a period that can rightly be called a period of anarchy, exploitation, tyranny, oppression, repression, and persecution. Non-Muslims had no rights during this period. In a way, the country's magistrates had become murderers.

During this same chaotic period, when the Lodi dynasty came to power, under the rule of Sikandar Lodi and Bahlol Khan, these dynasty's rulers witnessed heartbreaking and diabolical incidents of burning Hindus to death. While these may seem diabolical and heartbreaking to us today, they were joyous events for the ruling class of the time. The specter of communalism possessed them, which delighted them in the heartbreaking cries of Hindus dying in the fire.

Seeing such examples, we should consider that when Muslims were banning the practice of shaving the heads and beards of Hindus, they did not want anyone in their presence to be seen as a "kafir." They saw the beards, sacred threads, and tilaks of Hindus as something that made them assume that this person did not belong to them. This feeling of "*this person does not belong to us*" is the weak fiber of their psyche that teaches them to hate anyone who is different from Muslims.

Sadly, today's Muslims are also afflicted with this kind of thinking. They are unwilling to give up the values that have been ingrained in their minds for centuries.

This is why they still harbor hatred towards Hindus on communal grounds.

All such descriptions and facts make it clear that religion, i.e., sect, teaches people to hate each other. Because the basic nature of religion or sect is to teach destruction, to humiliate each other, to express hatred towards each other and to violate each other's rights.

A famous historical event dates back to 1499 AD. A Bengali Brahmin was doing commendable work in fostering unity between Hindus and Muslims. His teachings had led many Hindus and Muslims to become his disciples. He believed that both religions were true, showing humanity the path to God.

When Alexander learned of this Brahmin's views, he summoned his Islamic experts and consulted them. These radical Islamic scholars told Alexander that this viewpoint was completely wrong. They asked Alexander to choose between converting to Islam or being killed. Alexander did so. However, the Brahmin refused to change his faith, and he was executed.

Thus, the very Brahmin who truly created the Ganga-Jamuni culture was put to death by the sword of Islam. The truth is that the sword of Islam does not allow those who attempt to bring the truth of Ganga-Jamuni culture to reality. In reality, Ganga-Jamuni culture means that Hindus continue to silently endure oppression, while Islam continues to expand its ideology by adopting its autocratic nature.

A contemporary historian from Uttar Pradesh wrote,

"Lodhi was such a fanatic Muslim that he destroyed the places of worship of the infidels on a large scale. In Mathura, a major stronghold of idol worship, he completely destroyed the temples there. The idols installed there were given to butchers to use for weighing meat. He banned all Hindus from shaving their heads and beards. Thus, the entire city began to follow Islamic beliefs."(*Tarikh-e-Daudi*)

❒

*Chapter 7*

# Hindu Oppression During the Reign of Babur and Akbar

Burying India's history spanning millions of years deep, anti-Indian historians have singled out the Mughal period, presenting it as if today's India is a product of the Mughals' golden reign. Their efforts suggest that if the Mughal period were removed from India's history, India would have nothing to be proud of.

This is why the anti-Hindu oppressive actions of all Mughal rulers are forgotten and presented as if they dedicated their lives to India, Indianness, and Indians, and that their rule was a completely welfare state. Leftist historian Romila Thapar goes even further and says that the Mughals were not foreigners. Babur was a foreigner, but his descendants who came after him were completely Indian, because they were born in India. One truly pities the intelligence of historians like Romila Thapar. Because these are the same historians who still consider the *Aryans, Shakas, Huns, Kushans* (who were actually originally Indians), etc., who supposedly came to India centuries before Babur, to be foreigners. Even if they are considered foreigners, they were so assimilated into Indian society and culture that it is almost impossible to find them separately today. In fact, leftist historians like Romila Thapar repeatedly mention the Shakas and other peoples only to excuse the Mughals' sins or divert attention from their own.

It is unfortunate and ridiculous that even if these historians consider them foreigners, their descendants remain foreigners even today. Whereas the descendants of the Mughal ruler Babur became Indians immediately after his arrival in India (i.e., in 1530 AD, when Babur died and his son Humayun ascended the throne).

Babur, the founder of the Mughal dynasty, was the leader of a foreign plundering gang. When he arrived in India, he had nothing but plans to plunder India. This is why he plundered India extensively after his arrival. He also made every effort to culturally plunder India. During this invasion, his commander, Mir Baqi Khan, ordered the demolition of the world-famous Shri Ramchandra Temple in Ayodhya. This incident occurred in 1528 AD.

## Babar also wanted to become a Ghazi

Babar had a strong desire to become a Ghazi. In his victory letter, Babur described himself as the one who destroyed the foundations of idols. Only by doing so could he attain the sacred title of Ghazi. Earning this sacred title of Ghazi brought him the same peace that a staunch Muslim should. Anti-Hinduism and disrespect for Hindu religious sites were already ingrained in Babur as a culture. This was why, when the Ramchandra Temple in Ayodhya was demolished, Babur massacred thousands of Hindus. It is said that Hindus, hurt by the destruction of the temple, fiercely opposed Babur's army, in which a large number of Hindus sacrificed their lives.

Hindus fought nearly six dozen wars against Babur's atrocities over the past centuries, resulting in the sacrifice of millions of Hindus. After independence, despite all the facts, those who professed the religion of peace repeatedly attempted to deny that a Ram temple ever existed there. Their communal mindset and their complete devotion to communalism repeatedly prevented them from doing so. Shri Guru Gobind Singh Ji Maharaj, Maharani Raj Kunwari, and other great warriors and brave women also fought and sacrificed for this sacred site.

### Hindus have made incredible sacrifices for the temple

Like every Muslim emperor, Babur was fanatical and ruthless towards Hindus. In his first invasion of Bajaur, he massacred over 3,000 innocent Hindus. It is even said that during this battle, he had the heads of the dead Hindus cut off and erected as pillars on a platform. He committed similar massacres during his invasion of Bhera.

Babur was so driven by communal frenzy that he lost all sense of humanity. He was not Babur, but a 'barbarian,' demonstrating his barbarity at every step. Even if he achieved momentary success in establishing an empire based on fear by committing unprecedented atrocities against Hindus in India, this does not make him a great personality. The greatness of a person's actions must first be considered.

If someone's actions are considered "great" by a particular religion or sect, then even such so-called great deeds cannot be called humanitarian unless they are in keeping with humanitarian thinking and benefit all of humanity. What this means is that a person's actions can only be great if they embody a sense of inclusiveness, believe in equality of all sects; one-sided views cannot be considered great.

When Babur attacked Syedpur, Lahore, and Panipat, he massacred the elderly, children, and women. It is said that Guru Nanak witnessed these horrific atrocities with his own eyes. He called these attacks a "procession of sin" and Babur "Yamaraj."

Babur not only massacred Hindus to gain the sympathy of Muslims but also destroyed numerous Hindu religious sites. During his reign, a mosque was built in Sambhal by demolishing a temple. His commander, Sheikh Zaina, destroyed several temples in Chanderi.

Not only this, several Jain temples were also destroyed in Urwa, near Gwalior. Thus, by killing many simple and respectable people or destroying their places of worship, Babur attempted to declare himself a servant of Islam.

## Humayun and Akbar's Attitudes Towards Hindus

Babur's attitude towards Hindus was similar to that of his son, Humayun. Although he never succeeded in ruling permanently, he continued the same oppressive actions against Hindus as his father had, whenever and for as long as he remained emperor.

After Humayun, his son Akbar ascended the throne. His reign is considered highly auspicious for India by leftist and Congress historians. However, he, too, was never generous towards Hindus. The persecution of Hindus continued unabated during his reign. However, the country's first Prime Minister, Pandit Jawaharlal Nehru, and leftist historians have attempted to portray him as a liberal ruler. Considering his atrocities, the truth behind such writings by Pandit Jawaharlal Nehru and leftist historians is revealed. His contemporary historian, Ahmed Yadgar, says of Akbar:

"Bairam Khan bound the hands and feet of the unarmed and badly wounded Hindu king Hemu and took him to the young prince and said, 'Slay this infidel with your holy hands and accept the title of 'Ghazi'." The prince severed his head from his impure body. (November, 5 AD 1556) (*Tarikh-i-Afghan, Ahmad Yadgar, translated by Elliot and Dowson, Vol. VI, pp. 65-66*)

It is clear from this statement that Akbar killed Hemu with his own hands to obtain the title of 'Gazi'. He considered himself extremely fortunate that he had become a 'Gazi' at the age of 14.

'Gazi' means to prove oneself a true Muslim. 'Ghazi' means to declare oneself a killer of infidels and to rejoice in it. Ghazi also means to feel joy in destroying a Hindu.

Abul Fazl further wrote:

"Hemu's father was brought alive and presented before Nasir-ul-Malik, who ordered him to accept Islam, but the old man replied, 'I have worshipped my God for eighty years; How can I abandon my religion?'

Maulana Pari Mohammad ignored his reply and beheaded him with his sword." (*Akbarnama, Abul Fazal, Elliot and Dowson, p. 21*)

## Built a tall tower of severed heads of Hindus

Expressing his joy at this victory, Akbar built a tall tower of severed heads, so that ordinary Hindus would fear his rule. If Akbar were a ruler who believed in liberal and democratic values, he should never have done such a thing. On the contrary, he would have considered a policy of treating all his subjects equally and giving them equal justice, but he did not do so.

Furthermore, it is also true that on September 2, 1573, he built the tallest tower of heads ever built in Ahmedabad by beheading 2,000 Hindus. Thus, Akbar became obsessed with terrorizing Hindus and building towers from their heads, just as a drunkard becomes obsessed with clinking glasses every evening. These things are unbecoming of a ruler who believes in welfare policies and is concerned with the welfare of his subjects. Only a ruler who is adept at distinguishing between people from a religious perspective can do these things.

Those who consider Akbar great should definitely read his "*Akbarnama*" while considering his "great" deeds. According to the "*Akbarnama*," on March 3, 1575, during the conquest of Bengal, Akbar had so many soldiers and civilians killed that eight towers were built from their severed heads. By 1575, Akbar's reign in India had already completed 20 years. If Akbar had been inclined to dispense justice to all his subjects, he might have recovered after at least 20 years of rule. However, he failed and continued to delight in building a tower of severed Hindu heads. Akbar may have been liberal in his personal views, but his policy towards Hindus leads us to form the clear impression that he was a victim of religious fanaticism and hated Hindus because of his religious views.

## Rajput warriors were murdered

While Akbar's anti-Hindu policy may have been deliberately obscured in history, the truth is that he was completely anti-Hindu. Regarding Akbar's conquest of Chittor, Abul Fazal wrote- "On Akbar's orders, 8,000 Rajput warriors were first captured and later slaughtered."

Killing people during a war is a different matter, and war is considered justified only when it is waged for the attainment of justice. If it is done to oppress a particular community or to satisfy political desires, it cannot be considered justified. When such a war is being waged to massacre a particular community, it becomes completely illegal and anti-human. Those who believe in this type of warfare should then be considered murderers.

Thus, in our view, Akbar was simply a 'murderer.'

Abul Fazl further describes this:

"From morning till noon, another 40,000 peasants were also slaughtered, including 3,000 children and the elderly." (*Akbarnama, Abul Fazl, translated by H. Babbridge*)

This description of Akbar reveals that he was not only harsh towards the soldiers fighting against him, but also towards Hindu peasants and children. Clearly, the peasants and children were not fighting against him. Therefore, he should not have displayed any kind of harshness towards the peasants and children, demonstrating his supposed generosity.

## The Status of Hindu Women in Akbar's Harem

To fill his harem with Hindu women, Akbar forcibly married numerous Hindu princesses, but never allowed a Mughal woman to marry a Hindu. During Akbar's reign alone, 38 Rajput princesses were married into royal families: 12 to Akbar, 17 to Prince Salim, six to Daniyal, two to Murad, and one to Salim's son, Khusrau.

Akbar was a man of utter depravity. If judged against the yardstick of the essential qualities of a king in the tradition of Indian kings, he lacked a single kingly quality. The atrocities he committed against Hindu women, and the way he treated them as mere "farmworks" while crowding them into his harem, reveal a side of his character that allowed him to exploit Hindu women to his fullest, his lust and adultery. He even sought to make Queen Durgavati of Gondwana a victim of his lust.

This is mentioned by R.C. Majumdar in "*The Mughal Empire*," Volume 7. He writes:

"In 1564, Akbar attacked Rani Durgavati to satisfy his lust. However, after a valiant struggle, seeing her defeat imminent, the queen stabbed herself in the chest and committed suicide. However, her sister and daughter-in-law were captured and taken into Akbar's harem. At that time, Akbar was 22 years old, and Rani Durgavati was 40 years old." (*R.C. Majumdar, The Mughal Empire, Volume VII*)

In fact, Akbar inherited this attitude towards Hindu women from his religion, where even today it is believed that impregnating a Hindu girl entitles him to heaven. Therefore, this same thought was at work in Akbar's mind. This is why he organized Meena Bazaars to attract Hindu women to his harem. From there, he would arrange for his servants, soldiers, and sometimes even personally, to bring the Hindu woman of his choice.

## Adulterous Akbar and Hindu Society

Just imagine how inappropriate and insulting Hindu society must have considered such actions by the emperor at that time. Especially when respecting women and treating other people's sisters and daughters like one's own, daughters and mothers, has been an ancient tradition of Hindu society. How difficult would it have been for Hindu society to tolerate such an adulterous, hungry wolf? Especially when Hindu society had heard since ancient times that the king's sacred duty was to protect women and ensure that no cruel person could violate their dignity? Now, when they witnessed their own king beheading women, their pain was understandable.

Clearly, in such circumstances, the brave warriors of Hindu society would have been repeatedly tempted to rebel for the honor of their sisters and daughters. This is why the youth of these brave warriors never allowed any Mughal emperor, including Akbar, to sleep peacefully.

We should also keep in mind that when ordinary Hindu families saw their sisters and daughters falling prey to the emperor's lustful desires or witnessed such disrespectful behavior by his servants, their anger would have been directed at ordinary Mughal officials or Muslims. Just as we saw the people of India raging against the British before independence. In those circumstances, Hindus would have attacked ordinary Muslims or officials, seeing them as representatives of Akbar or any Mughal emperor. This is what spread the flames of rebellion.

This fire of rebellion should be called communal riots in today's context. Because these rebellions were violence fueled by the communal ideology of the government. At that time, these riots were patronized by communal rulers. Consequently, contemporary historians would write about the riots according to the wishes of their political leaders. The truth behind the events that drove Hindus to repeatedly rebel against Muslim rulers was never written.

## What are communal riots?

In reality, riots are violence instigated against the communal thinking of a particular community. When one group refuses to tolerate this, anger unleashes unbridled. We see this even today. If we consider the reasons behind the frequent communal riots in cities like Meerut, we find that when Muslim boys make it difficult for Hindu sisters and daughters to walk through their streets and even resort to indecent and inappropriate behavior against them, the blood of some Hindu youth boils.

Then we see that this feeling of revenge takes the form of communal riots. Congress and left-wingers interpret and define these communal riots as if Hindus were the most at fault among the two communities. Their policy of Muslim appeasement prevents the truth from coming to light. Otherwise, if they had the courage to admit the truth, they should clearly state that no community, especially the Muslim community, will behave in an indecent manner towards Hindu sisters and daughters, and if anyone is found to be doing so, strict action will be taken against them.

## The Meaning of 'Stain on the Back'

Even today, we see a proverb prevalent in our Hindu society: "I have a stain on my back." Members of our Hindu society use it when they have suffered a humiliating incident. They feel no peace until they avenge that humiliating incident. In fact, this proverb dates back to the time of Alauddin Khilji. Alauddin Khilji first established the tradition of branding a royal mark on the back of a horse if a Hindu ruler accepted his suzerainty. This would indicate that the king riding that horse was a slave of Alauddin Khilji.

Our kings and brave warriors never accepted this stigma lightly. They were determined to erase it. Later, Indians established it as a proverb for the times of other Muslim rulers. This proverb was actually a Hindu's unquestionable resolve. They would devote their lives to fulfilling that resolve. What this means is that in a Hindu society deeply ingrained in the tradition of washing away the stain on one's back, how could they tolerate any insulting behavior by Muslims? It is clear that every insulting action sparked a wave of resistance, which would eventually take the form of rebellion or communal riots. History has not accurately depicted this sentiment and emotion.

Why did communal riots occur in India? If this is considered objectively and that reflection is placed in history with utmost honesty, then the fact about India will become clear: communal riots began since the arrival of Muslims here, and if they still occur today, the main reason behind them is the abuse of Muslims towards the sisters and daughters of Hindu society.

Although Congress and leftist historians try to tell us that there was no history of riots in India before independence, they try to ignore all the sins of the Muslim era, due to which thousands, if not millions, of our Hindus had to lose their lives at that time.

## A great misfortune for the country

Indeed, the country's misfortune is that Akbar, the adulterer who insulted Hindu sisters and daughters, is considered the greatest ruler of this country. Today's Akbars, who follow him, have become obsessed with achieving greatness: uplift Hindu sisters and daughters and be called great like Akbar.

We also learn about Akbar that after Akbar's murder of Prince Jaimal, his brave wife was about to commit *sati* on horseback to protect her honor. When the evil eye of the adulterous Akbar fell on that beautiful warrior woman, Akbar intercepted her on the way. He sent her relatives, who were on their way to the cremation ground, to rot in prison, and stuffed the princess into his harem.

Such sinful acts establish Akbar as a villain of history. He never showed even the slightest respect for women. He tried to cross every limit of meanness and cruelty. Abul Fazal described Akbar's harem thus:

"Akbar's harem consisted of five thousand women, and these five thousand women were separate from his 36 wives. A tavern was built near the emperor's palace. So many prostitutes gathered there that it became difficult to count them. If any courtier wanted to take a new girl home, he had to seek Akbar's permission. Sometimes, quarrels broke out among people over who could take beautiful women. Once, Akbar himself summoned some prostitutes and asked them who had sex with them first."

According to Islamic Sharia, non-Muslims living in any Muslim state had to pay a price, known as Jizya, to protect their property and women from being taken away.

In fact, the Jizya tax was a cruel policy of the government that instilled a sense of humiliation among Hindus at that time, which Hindu society was unable to accept *(Muntakhab-ut-Tawarikh: Abdul Qadir Badayuni, Volume II, page 383, translated by V. Smith, Akbar the Great Mughal, page 108).*

We have numerous other similar examples, facts, and evidence that clearly demonstrate that no Mughal, including Akbar, supported a liberal approach or policy towards Hindus. For him, religion came first. He considered it appropriate to rule based on communal thinking.

Even if Akbar is portrayed as a lover of India and a Hindu, this entire propaganda is solely aimed at defaming and insulting Hindu society. The adverse effect on the current young generation of the country is that the more Akbar's so-called liberalism is imposed on the new generation, the more they become mentally impotent. He sees faults in Maharana Pratap and purity everywhere in the greatness of Akbar.

## The Trick of Leftist Historians

In reality, this shift in perspective has been the sole objective of leftist and Congress historians. Congress has spread this kind of propaganda to serve its own political interests. It has considered it its right to continue ruling the country through Muslim appeasement. Following Congress's example, leftists have also considered it their sacred duty to curse Hindus, Hindutva, and India. By doing so, they too believe that one day they will bring this country under the "red flag."

While the current Muslim leadership, realizing the folly of both, and seeing their own population growing in the country, has now begun plotting to seize power. Their argument for this is that they have ruled India for 800 years and made the greatest sacrifices for its independence, therefore, they will rule India in the future.

The sacrifices of all sacrifices have been erased from history, and those who betrayed the country have become great heroes. Today, let us consider this testimony of history: our great India, which our ancestors emphasized.

Muslim communal elements exploit the anti-national sentiments of Congress and leftist historians by claiming that the Red Fort and the Taj Mahal were built by us. Hindus have no say here. Therefore, if the country's past was ours, the future will also be ours. While there is democracy in the country, Muslims are plotting to take this democracy hostage based on their growing population. Behind all these plans, communal thinking is at work. If we contemplate the future of India, religious thinking appears to be clouding India's future as well.

Certainly, necessary steps are needed to save the country from civil war. For this, truly peace-loving Hindu and Muslim leadership should come together. They should unanimously demand a Uniform Civil Code and population control. These people should put pressure on the government so that all the people of the country get equal rights and everyone should work together for the development of the country.

❐

*Chapter 8*

# Jahangir, Shah Jahan, and Aurangzeb's Hindu Policy

Akbar is said to have had a majority of his army composed of Hindus, whom he trusted immensely. These Hindus in Akbar's army are often seen as linked to Akbar's so-called secularism, in order to instill in the reader the belief that Akbar was truly a great ruler who believed in love, non-violence, and brotherhood. For him, there was no such thing as religion that could divert him from his royal duty.

In fact, such a narrative about Akbar is very misleading, because the reality was quite the opposite. For Akbar, a Kafir was a Kafir, and a Muslim was a Muslim, although he considered himself far superior to ordinary Muslims. Scholars also believe that he wanted to declare himself a second prophet. This statement by Badayuni, revealing Akbar's communal thinking towards Hindus, makes a lot of sense:

"When the battle was going on in Haldighati, and the Rajputs of Akbar's army and those of Rana Pratap's army were fighting each other, and it was becoming impossible to distinguish who was on which side, I asked my commander of the royal army who he should shoot at - so that only the enemy would die."

Then Asaf Khan, the commander of his army, replied that it does not matter who gets shot, because the fighters on both sides are infidels. Whoever gets shot will die, and Islam will only benefit." (*Muntakhab-ut-Tawarikh: Abdul Qadir Badayuni, Volume II, trans. Akbar*)

(*The Great Mughal: V. Smith, reprinted 1962; History and Culture of the Indian People, The Mughal Empire: R.C. Majumdar, Volume VII, page 132, 3rd edition*)

## Jahangir's Policy Towards Hindus

Akbar's attitude towards Hindus was such only because he too was pursuing the goal of Darul Islam. He was also influenced and obsessed with the idea that the entire world should be colored by Islam and the earth should be purified of infidels. This was why he destroyed Hindus to his heart's content during his reign. We learn about this attitude towards Hindus from his own son, Jahangir. Jahangir wrote in his biography, '*Tarikh-i-Salimshahi*,' that- "five to six hundred thousand Hindus were slaughtered during the reigns of Akbar and Jahangir." (*Tarikh-i-Salim Shahi, trans. Price, pp. 225-26*)

There are many other similar examples that make it clear that, like Akbar, his son, Salim, nicknamed Jahangir, also exhibited cruelty and harshness towards Hindus during his reign.

Historians who distort history may have portrayed Jahangir as a kind and just ruler, but Smith describes him as "a strange combination of gentleness and cruelty, justice and righteousness, refinement and brutality, good sense and childishness."

Salim was the first to express the sentiment of rebellion against his father during Akbar's reign. Later, rebellion against each Mughal emperor by his son became a 'great tradition' of Mughal rule. When Salim alias Jahangir, who had rebelled against his own father, had to face the rebellion of his son Khusro, he pardoned him for the first time, but after the rebellion for the second time, he blinded his son Khusro.

In fact, the reason for such rebellions by sons during Mughal rule was largely due to their fathers' debauchery. All the lecherous and adulterous Mughal rulers abducted Hindu women and made them their concubines or queens. Fearing that their illegitimate children might become contenders for power, or sensing their potential threat, they orchestrated power-grabbing conspiracies in the royal palaces. The tree grows as the seed and bears the same fruit. Where there is a lack of values, there is a high probability of producing uncultured children.

Our ancient sages established the monogamous system because if too many wives were kept, or if the king was lecherous, adulterous, or addicted, there would be power struggles among his many children, which would have a negative impact on the citizens of the kingdom. As long as this Vedic system remained in effect, there was no trouble or problem anywhere. As soon as the Vedic system began to decay, suffering spread everywhere. Even among the common people, there is only one reason for property disputes: today's so-called kings, our representatives, are caught up in power intrigues and property disputes.

## The Influence of the Mughals on Indian Society

The Mughal rule has had a profound impact on Indian society.

It is a different matter that this influence of Mughal rule is most visible in creating negative ideologies and environments, which have led to the deception of human society. No matter how much effort was made to make the licentious rulers of the Mughal period, who behaved completely contrary to the Aryan tradition, revered as rulers of the country, they do not even fall into the lowest category of the excellence of the Indian Aryan tradition. Regarding the Mughal rulers, any Muslim ruler, or the British, it should be understood that the aim of these foreign invaders was to forcibly impose their rule not only on India but also on all the countries outside India that were under their control. Their aim was not to teach morality to any country or community or to prove themselves more useful to the world by becoming humanitarians.

While India's Rajdharma considers ruling others in an immoral and illegal manner as inappropriate and completely prohibited, it believes in liberation from subjugation. The sages of India established the state system to liberate people from all forms of exploitation, oppression, repression, and tyranny. However, whenever and wherever Muslim and Christian rulers established their power in the name of religion, they violated the rights of others and committed the immoral and inhuman act of forcibly imposing their rule on them. History should describe such acts of theirs in this manner.

When one community commits inhuman atrocities and another tolerates them, communal riots erupt, causing great harm to humanity. This is what fosters feelings of rebellion among the oppressed groups against the oppressor. If feelings of rebellion continued to grow among Indians against the Ottoman, Mughal, and later the British, it was only because their rule had become a symbol of inhuman behavior in India.

## Examples of Jahangir's Policy towards Hindus

Another example of Jahangir's intolerance towards Hindus is that he severely punished Hindus living in the Rajouri region of Jammu for marrying Muslim women. During his lifetime, when Jahangir succeeded in hoisting his victory flag on the Kangra Fort, he had a cow slaughtered there to celebrate his victory, in order to humiliate the Hindu king and his Hindu subjects. Not only this, he had the images of Hindu deities inside the Varaha temple destroyed and thrown into a nearby pond.

When Jahangir fought against the Portuguese, he closed all Christian churches. Thus, he demonstrated his religious intolerance against every non-Muslim. Similarly, Guru Arjun Dev of the Sikhs was persecuted because he carried the flag of Hinduism and worked for Hindu awakening. Jahangir did not want the entire Hindu community to rise under Guruji's leadership and for the Mughal rule to be overthrown in the storm of nationalism in this country. Those who today propagate the false narrative that there was never any animosity between Mughals and Sikhs should seriously read and understand these facts so that they can be brainwashed. The history of those anti-national historians who have created differences and distance between Hindus and Sikhs by presenting false historical facts is a wastebasket.

This was the reason why he inflicted countless atrocities on Guruji and his followers. It's not that Jahangir persecuted only Hindus; his cruelty continued unabated against other sects as well. In India, Sikhs, Jains, and Buddhists are considered branches of the Hindu Vedic religion. Legally, the British even accepted these three as descendants of the same patriarch, thus bringing them under the umbrella of Hinduism. Demonstrating this same communal anti-Hindu policy, Jahangir once ordered all followers of Jainism to leave Gujarat.

## Shah Jahan's Anti-Hindu Policy

Jahangir's son, Shah Jahan, succeeded him. Many leftist historians in India have described Shah Jahan's reign as a golden age. However, there was nothing truly worthy of such a claim. The claim that Shah Jahan commissioned the Taj Mahal to be built in the name of his wife, Mumtaz Mahal, is also a myth. The reality is that anti-Hindu extremism was deeply ingrained in the Mughal emperor's very being. Shah Jahan's debauchery was even greater than that of his predecessors. He did not even spare his own daughter, Jahanara, to satisfy his lust. This daughter resembled her mother, Mumtaz.

It is said that during Akbar's reign, a rule was enacted that no Mughal princess would be married. Consequently, all Mughal princesses would engage in illicit relationships with courtiers and even servants to satisfy their sexual desires. The Mughal emperor made every effort to ensure that his daughter, Jahanara, would not fall in love with anyone, so that she would remain his. Jahanara also fully assisted in the perpetuation of the debauched emperor's debauchery. She would lure Hindu girls into her trap and bring them before her debauched father, Emperor Shah Jahan.

With Jahanara's assistance, Shah Jahan raped the wife of Mumtaz's brother, Shaista Khan, several times.

It is also said that Jahanara lured the 13-year-old Brahmin girl, who was Shah Jahan's royal astrologer, into her palace, tricked her into drugging her, and handed her over to her father. Shah Jahan married her in his 58th year. The innocent 13-year-old girl had resisted the lust of this lecherous king, but nothing worked. Her father was left heartbroken.

Later, after Shah Jahan's imprisonment, this same Brahmin girl poured acid on her face with her own hands to escape Aurangzeb and prevent herself from falling prey to his lust once again. Truly, this was a remarkable act of courage on the part of the girl, who made such a drastic decision to protect her honor and chastity, escaping the clutches of the executioner emperor. This so-called lecherous emperor, a worshipper of beauty, condemned many beautiful women to a hellish life. It is said that his harem contained 8,000 women. Most of these women were from Hindu families.

## Shah Jahan named himself Timur II

Shah Jahan also named himself Timur II. The sole reason behind this was that he considered Timur II's cruelty and ruthlessness his role model and adopted the same behavior and attitude towards Hindus in his practical life. He enjoyed calling himself Timur II. This fact is revealed in "*The Legacy of Muslim Rule in India*," by Dr. K.S. Lal, 1992, page 132. By doing this, Shah Jahan proved his devout Muslimness. He not only convinced his Muslim brothers that he was a devout Muslim and that becoming a Ghazi would bring him as much joy as any other Muslim. On the contrary, he also signaled to Hindus that if they did not accept Islam, they should be prepared to accept the sword.

When religious authorization to indulge in carnal pleasures with Hindu women was given, and when the spirit of treating them as their own possessions was obsessed with the idea of treating them as their own, what Muslim in his youth would not want to enjoy all this? Indeed, from his teenage years, Shah Jahan was completely filled with hatred for Hindus, meaning infidels.

Historians have written that- "As a prince, Shah Jahan captured Fatehpur Sikri and carried out a horrific massacre of Hindus in the city of Agra."

Surely the prince did this only to experience the pleasure of massacring the infidels, so that he could become a Ghazi and get the right to go to heaven.

At that time, a wealthy Italian man named Della Valle visited India. He wrote many memoirs that shed light on contemporary history. He wrote about Shah Jahan,

"Shah Jahan's army displayed terrible barbarity. Hindu citizens were forced to give up their accumulated wealth through severe torture, and many noble Hindu women of high birth were raped." (*Keynes Handbook for Visitors to Agra and Its Neighborhood, page 25*)

The Badshahnama states:

"His Majesty the Emperor was informed that in Banaras, a major Hindu center, the reconstruction of many temples had begun during the reign of his father, and that the infidel Hindus were now nearing completion.

The Emperor, the protector of Islam, ordered the demolition of all temples under construction in Banaras and elsewhere throughout his kingdom.

Information was received from the Allahabad region that seventy-six temples in the Banaras district had been demolished." (*Badshahnama: Abdul Hamid Lahori, translated by Elliot and Dowson, Volume VII, page 36*)

"The practice of desecrating and destroying Hindu temples assumed a systematic, monstrous form during the reign of Shah Jahan." (*Medieval India, Harishchandra Verma, page 141*)

"While returning from Kashmir in 1632, Shah Jahan was informed that many women who had been converted to Islam had reconverted to Hinduism and married into Hindu families.

Historical researchers conclude that "on the Emperor's orders, all these Hindus were taken captive. First, they were all fined so high that none of them could pay.

They were then given the choice between accepting Islam and death. All the men who refused to convert were beheaded. Approximately four thousand five hundred women were forcibly converted to Islam and sent to the harems of generals, officers, and the emperor's close associates and relatives." (*History and Culture of the Indian People, R.C. Majumdar, Bharatiya Vidya Bhavan, page 312*)

In 1657, Shah Jahan fell ill, and his son, Aurangzeb, imprisoned him in the Agra Fort along with his concubine, Jahanara. Aurangzeb, acting as an ideal son, understanding his father's sexuality, allowed him to keep 40 concubines. Upon arriving in Delhi, he placed a select few of his father's thousands of concubines in his harem and expelled the rest from the fort.

It is said that the thousands of women driven away by Aurangzeb also found refuge in the same part of Delhi that is today known as GB Road, the red light area of Delhi. Thus, this area of GB Road became a symbol of peace and the establishment of a golden age in India. Shah Jahan's contribution is sufficient to explain the plight of women during his reign even today. While historians have falsely attributed the Taj Mahal and the Red Fort to Shah Jahan, no one has shown the moral courage to clarify the truth: what continues to happen on GB Road to this day is also Shah Jahan's contribution.

Shah Jahan died in the Agra Fort on January 22, 1666, at the age of 74, according to The History Channel, due to an overdose of aphrodisiacs.

Aurangzeb's Terrorist Reign Aurangzeb holds a place in history as one of the cruelest Mughal emperors. He crossed all limits of religious cruelty and ruthlessness towards Hindus. However, leftist and Muslim historians consider him one of India's most liberal rulers, and efforts have been made to downplay his cruelty and ruthlessness in comparison to his so-called generosity. This Mughal ruler ruled from 1658 to 1707 AD. He made every effort to give his entire political system an Islamic touch. This is why he even named his law "*Fatwa-e-Alamgiri*." This law, called "*Fatwa-e-Alamgiri*," incorporated all the provisions of Sharia law that gave the ruler free rein to oppress non-Muslims. Despite these provisions of "Fatwa-e-Alamgiri," historians who have attempted to portray Aurangzeb's rule as a boon for India are truly pitiable.

Aurangzeb, ruling according to his Sharia law system, severely restricted the rights of non-Muslims. With the implementation of this system, Muslims gained numerous rights, such as the forcible seizure of Hindu property and the enslavement of women. In order to oppress and convert Hindus,

Aurangzeb unleashed untold atrocities on his non-Muslim subjects. They were treated unequally. Muslims were granted certain privileges, while the fundamental rights of non-Muslims were violated. From 1665, Hindu traders were charged double the customs duty, while Muslim traders were exempted from the duty. In 1679, Aurangzeb imposed the "Zanziya" tax on Hindus. This Jizya tax was essentially a tool for draining Hindus, imposed by every Muslim king or sultan during their reign. It was implemented with even greater ruthlessness during Aurangzeb's reign. So that the blood would be squeezed from their very bones, that is, their economic, social, and political life system would be completely destroyed and all paths to progress would be blocked.

Aurangzeb also kept a close watch on his officials, so that they could not show any leniency towards his Hindu subjects. If any official was found to be lenient towards Hindus, he was subjected to severe torture. Subjecting Hindus to religious persecution, Aurangzeb banned the celebration of all their religious festivals. Hindus could no longer celebrate any religious festival, including Diwali. He also stopped Hindu religious ceremonies. Not only this, in order to instill a feeling of inferiority among the Hindu people, Aurangzeb even took away their right to sit in palanquins or ride elephants and Arabian horses.

## Destroyed Religious Places

Aurangzeb also showed a keen interest in destroying Hindu religious places. He wanted to transform India into Darul Islam. From this perspective, Hindu religious sites were like thorns in his eyes. To achieve this objective, Aurangzeb made the destruction of Hindu religious sites a part of his government policy.

On September 12, 1667, he issued a royal decree ordering the demolition of the Kalkaji Temple in Delhi. Accounts from contemporary writers and historians indicate that on April 9, 1669, he ordered the demolition of all Hindu temples and schools in his kingdom. The sole purpose of this was to ensure that Hindus, unable to access their religious sites, would sooner or later be forced to embrace Islam. This would facilitate the rapid spread of Islam throughout India. Furthermore, another reason for the destruction of Hindu religious sites was the belief that God, or Allah, resides in mosques, not temples, and that the Quran's method of attaining Him is the ultimate truth. Furthermore, if a person of another religion offers their religious prayers, it is completely inappropriate.

## The famous temple in Mathura was demolished

Aurangzeb was well aware of how his ancestor, Babur, had demolished the temple of Shri Ramchandra Ji, the great hero of Indian history, in Ayodhya in 1528 AD. Now, to gain popularity among Muslims, he conceived the idea of demolishing the magnificent temple of Shri Krishna in Mathura. He could also earn the same merit as his ancestor Babur had by demolishing the temple of Shri Ramchandra Ji.

To achieve this objective, Aurangzeb destroyed the famous Keshav Rai temple in Mathura in January 1670 and built a mosque there. This incident has been described as a minor incident in history, whereas, after the demolition of Shri Ramchandra Ji's temple in Ayodhya, it was a very significant event in Indian history. The people of India held immense reverence for these two great heroes of Indian history, Shri Ramchandra Ji and Shri Krishna Ji, and worshipped them as gods.

The Hindu psyche of the country has never forgotten this humiliating treatment meted out to these two historical heroes by the Mughal emperors. It has repeatedly expressed its anger and resentment, and whenever it has the opportunity, it has spared no effort to express its anger and resentment against Muslims.

Hindus were filled with a sense of humiliation and contempt, and they never failed to express it time and again. While the wicked historians have never mentioned these atrocities committed by the Mughal emperors, they have repeatedly attempted to portray Hindu anger and resentment as communal resentment. The truth is that the Hindu masses, oppressed by the Mughals' humiliating behavior, expressed their anger and frustration through their anger and frustration, leading to a continuous cycle of communal riots in the country.

The Indian public has held immense reverence for the Shri Vishwanath Temple in Varanasi since ancient times. Aurangzeb was determined to destroy this supreme center of Hindu faith.

Because he always planned to hurt Hindus, causing them extreme distress. Consequently, shortly after the destruction of the Mathura temple, he also ordered the demolition of the Shri Vishwanath Temple in Varanasi and the famous Somnath Temple. The destruction of the Kashi Vishwanath Temple left the Hindu population extremely restless. They repeatedly attempted to avenge this insult.

In the view of leftist and Congress historians, Aurangzeb, the liberal emperor of India, also subjected the Hindu population of Rajasthan to religious persecution. Approximately 300 Hindu temples in the Udaipur and Marwar regions of Rajasthan fell victim to his religious policies. Consequently, he issued a royal decree in 1679, deciding to demolish all these Hindu temples. Many Hindus sacrificed their lives protecting Hindu temples, but they could not withstand the ruthless sword of the cruel Aurangzeb for long. As a result, the emperor's soldiers succeeded in vandalizing and destroying all these temples. Sixty-three temples in Chittor were demolished on Aurangzeb's orders.

## Temples were destroyed everywhere

An examination of Aurangzeb's reign and his religious policy reveals that he considered every possible means to render India devoid of Hindus and Hindu religious sites. He roamed various regions of India at that time, hunting like a temple-eater. Wherever he learned of a religious site established by a particular Hindu great man, he would descend upon it like a hissing serpent and destroy it.

Following this policy, Aurangzeb issued a government order on June 1, 1681, to completely destroy the sacred Jagannath Temple in Orissa. Those who opposed Aurangzeb's order were put to death by the sword. Furthermore, they were subjected to all the atrocities that are considered justifiable in Islam for attaining the position of Ghazi or serving Islam.

Even the Hindu religious sites of South India were not spared from Aurangzeb's wrath. In September 1681, when Aurangzeb decided to embark on a campaign to the South to further his supposed victories, he issued orders to his soldiers and generals to destroy all Hindu religious sites along the route and to ruthlessly kill any infidels who opposed him. In September 1682, he also issued an order to demolish the famous Bindu-Madhav Temple in Banaras.

Thus, demonstrating his religious fanaticism, Aurangzeb destroyed numerous Hindu temples in India and built mosques in their place. He felt a deep sense of joy in destroying Hindu religious sites, a feeling he repeatedly sought to satisfy. He considered himself a servant of Islam. There was no greater service to Islam than destroying the religious sites of infidels and forcibly converting them to Islam, thus spreading and expanding Islam. To prove himself a servant of Islam, he made this service his life's vow.

## Aurangzeb remains a villain in the eyes of Hindus

This is why he remains a highly regarded ruler in the eyes of followers of Islam, while in the eyes of those Hindus who endured his atrocities, he remains a staunch, intolerant, and tyrannical ruler. In India, one section considers Aurangzeb a historical hero, while another considers him a historical villain. This difference in perspective has also led to communal riots in India.

Aurangzeb was ostracized by the Hindu society of that time. A feeling of hatred towards him was widespread. Be it the Sikhs of Punjab (we have deliberately omitted Aurangzeb's atrocities against the Sikh Gurus of Punjab, as there is much to be learned about his policies towards the Sikhs) or the Ahom rulers of Assam, everyone harbored a deep hatred for him. This deep hatred was not merely based on communal grounds, but also because the people of Punjab and Assam felt bound by a common national tradition. If a thorn pricked someone in Assam, the people of Punjab felt the pain, and similarly, the people of Assam felt the suffering of the people of Punjab. Because of this national sentiment, Aurangzeb never received the honor of being a national hero. Surely, his soul yearns to receive this honor even today.

Although leftist and Congress historians, understanding his anguish, have made every effort to establish him as a national hero or Bharat Ratna, the people of the country are still unwilling to accept him as a national hero.

Those who attempted to establish Aurangzeb as a historical or national hero and accepted him as such succeeded in establishing their own country. Even today, those who consider Aurangzeb their historical or national hero are preparing to establish a new country. Wherever Hindus are being oppressed or forced to migrate, those with Aurangzeb-like thinking have been seen succeeding in establishing their dominance.

Thus, Aurangzeb was a symbol of fragmentation, division, and disintegration throughout his life, and even after his death, he remains a symbol of fragmentation, division, and disintegration. People like Sir Syed Ahmed Khan, who carried forward this thinking, were the first to talk about bi-nationalism in the country.

## Hindu national heroes mounted a massive protest

At that time, numerous Hindu leaders, including Shivaji, Guru Tegh Bahadur, Guru Gobind Singh, and Banda Veer Bairagi, stood up to Aurangzeb's policies. They were welcomed and honored by the people of the country. No matter how much historians have corrupted the historical tradition, the reverence that Hindus still hold for Shivaji and Banda Veer Bairagi makes it easy to imagine how Hindu society at that time respected these two historical heroes and how brave they must have displayed in the face of Islamic atrocities against the Hindu population.

Displaying similar bravery, Guru Gobind Singh sacrificed his four sons. Guru Tegh Bahadur sacrificed his own life, while Shivaji took on the task of ending the Mughal Empire.

It is no less surprising that just 30 years after Aurangzeb's death, Shivaji's successors succeeded in virtually eliminating the Mughal dynasty and establishing their rule over a large part of present-day India. It would be no exaggeration to call this event of 1737 the country's first independence.

In reality, this success achieved by Hindus through the efforts of the Gurus of Punjab and the successors of the brave Shivaji was a victory over the Mughals' history filled with violence. This has not been properly given its true meaning and context in our history.

## Tipu Sultan, the Aurangzeb of South India

Left-wing historians have attempted to portray even a religiously intolerant, fanatic ruler like Tipu Sultan as secular. The truth is that he was the Aurangzeb of South India in terms of persecuting Hindus. He persecuted millions of Hindus during his reign. Demonstrating his religious intolerance and fanaticism, Tipu Sultan converted millions of Hindus to Islam. Like Aurangzeb, Tipu Sultan destroyed numerous Hindu temples, which makes it impossible to say that he was a tolerant and liberal ruler towards Hindus.

In 2015, the RSS mouthpiece, '*Panchjanya*,' published an article to this effect, in which, in protest of Tipu Sultan's birth anniversary, he was described as the Aurangzeb of the South, who forcibly converted millions of people.

Foreign scholars have also written about Tipu Sultan's fanaticism and religious intolerance. Their references and facts make it clear that, like other Muslim rulers, he, too, advocated a policy of harshness towards Hindus.

In the 19th century, British government official and author William Logan wrote in his book "*Malabar Manual*" that- "Tipu Sultan, with his army of 30,000 soldiers, wreaked havoc in Calicut. Tipu Sultan hanged men and women in public places, and their children were hung by tying them around their necks. In this book, William also made several allegations against Tipu Sultan, including the destruction of temples and churches, and forced marriages.

The book "*Life of Tipu Sultan*," published in 1964, states that the Sultan forced more than 100,000 Hindus and more than 70,000 Christians in the Malabar region to convert to Islam.

❒

## *Chapter 9*

# Religion and the Crusade Wars

In the name of religion, bloody conflicts have erupted between Christians, Jews, and Muslims, causing immense harm to humanity. Millions of people either lost their lives in these wars or were forced to flee. Large numbers of people were converted, and those who refused to convert were subjected to inhuman and diabolical atrocities. Humanity itself groans at the horrors of this.

Note that both Christianity and Islam call themselves religions of peace and pat themselves on the back for having taught the world civilization and culture. They also claim to have established humanity and human values in the world and to have a glorious past for all these things. Yet, they shy away from taking responsibility for the 300-year-long destruction they have inflicted on humanity. Although this is a harsh truth of history, those who chant, "*Religion does not teach us to hate each other*," must read and understand the immense destruction caused by these Crusades.

According to Wikipedia, the wars fought by European Christians between 1095 and 1291 AD in an attempt to wrest Palestine, the holy land of their religion, and the Church of Jesus's Tomb in its capital, Jerusalem, from Muslims and take control of it are known as the Crusades, Christian Crusades,

Crusades, or the Wars of the Cross. Historians recognize seven such Wars of the Cross.

## The Location of the City of Jerusalem

There was a large church in Jerusalem, built in the fourth century by the mother of Constantine, the first Christian emperor of Rome, near the Tomb of Jesus.

In fact, whether Jerusalem or any other historical site, all of them were under the rule of Aryan kings at one time or another. When the rule, administration, and discipline of the Aryan kings weakened, various sects began to flourish here. Later, when this region came under the Christian rule, they established their own religious sites in their own way.

When this region became part of the Roman Empire, its rulers converted to Christianity from the fourth century. For the next 300 years, Christians ruled the region in their own way, governing society based on their religious customs and beliefs. Later, when Islam was established in 610 AD, it signaled a threat to Christianity and other world religions and their powers, as this religion had already begun to spread and expand its reach. This was bound to lead to a clash between these two religions. In the seventh century, Islam began to pursue its expansionist plans with great intensity. The Prophet's successors, the Caliphs, began achieving unexpected success in establishing their rule over neighboring and distant lands. This boosted their morale, and their desire for plunder and robbery grew stronger. When this Muslim force, committing sectarian atrocities in the name of Islam, advanced towards Palestine, it took only 10 years to subjugate it.

## The Initial Stage of the Conflict

Thus, this holy Christian shrine fell under Muslim control. For some time, Muslims did not pose any significant obstacles to Jews performing their worship at this shrine, but gradually, as they established dominance throughout the region, this situation changed in the 11th century. When Muslims significantly increased their population, they began to threaten the Jews. It has always been a characteristic of Muslims that when they are in small numbers in a particular region, they remain pacifists, but as their numbers increase, they make life difficult for those of the opposite faith.

During this time, the Seljuk Turks significantly increased their power from the Caspian Sea to Jerusalem. The Seljuks conquered Palestine, along with several other countries, and by 1071 AD, Jerusalem and its holy sites were under their control. As Muslims tightened their sectarian grip on these places, the result was that Christian travel became difficult and fraught with danger.

At that time, the Normans were the rulers of England. They already held sway over a portion of France. Around 1070 AD, they further increased their power by conquering the island of Sicily from the Muslims. They also succeeded in annexing the adjoining southern Italy. As a result, the Mediterranean, which had been under pressure from Muslim rulers in North Africa, opened up to Christians at this time.

In 395 AD, the Roman Empire was divided into two parts. The capital of the western part was Rome. This empire was broken up in 476 AD by the invasion of the northern barbarians. The eastern part of Christendom had its capital in Constantinople (Istanbul), and Greek emperors ruled there. In addition to Eastern Europe, their empire also extended to Asia Minor. The Turks had conquered most of Asia Minor, leaving only the area near the capital and some coastal areas under the control of the Roman (Greek) emperor. The emperor sought the assistance of Western Christians in this crisis. The Pope of Rome himself was keen to liberate the Holy Land from the Turks.

Indeed, this kind of thinking and approach of Christian and Muslim rulers reveals that they were engaged in conspiratorial schemes to seize each other's lands and property. Their motives were not public interest, but rather self-interest and monetary gain. This kind of selfishness undoubtedly leads to great destruction. Whenever communal kings have played such selfish games based on communalism, humanity has faced massive destruction. Now, when the rulers of Christianity and Islam were engaged in such games, the stage was being set for a major catastrophe between them as well.

Preachers who spewed venom against each other on communal grounds also played a significant role in making this situation explosive. Peter the monk, a resident of Amiya, began inciting the public to wage a religious war in France and Italy. This preacher's objective was certainly to incite a clash between the two communities on communal grounds. His intention was to destroy the sect called Islam. Meanwhile, Islamic preachers had long been inciting their followers to such a situation.

Through the efforts of Christian missionaries, six hundred thousand Crusaders were willing to sacrifice their lives in the name of religion. However, the division of Christians between the Eastern and Western empires profoundly influenced these Crusades, as this division persisted for a long time.

## The First Crusade

Religious fanaticism casts a deep darkness over a person's mind. It first extinguishes the lamp of reason. Just as a thief shuts off the source of light before entering a house, religion does the same by covering a person's mind with a veil of ignorance.

Inspired by this mentality, people went to war in the name of religion, becoming frenzied, rebellious, and extremist. The Christian missionary Peter and his companions enraged the people to such an extent that millions left their homes to destroy heretics, infidels, or those of the opposite faith. The ghost of religion was so powerful that no one had any time to think about humanism.

As for political power, it too had become so tainted with communalism that it saw development only in destruction. Inspired by the Pope and St. Peter, millions of citizens from France, Germany, and Italy, along with their children, loaded their belongings onto carts and set off by land towards the Holy Land in March 1096. Faith itself became the cause of destruction. This situation tells us that when a person's faith and devotion to human values are shaken, they begin to see development only in destruction.

This is why our great sages, their ancestors, considered religion and humanity together, symbolizing love, as useful for the world, and considered their propagation and expansion the greatest duty of humanity. This interdependent relationship between humanity and religion was shattered by the demon of religion, because religion's only purpose is to divide. Consequently, humanity and religion fell into the clutches of the demon of religion.

When religion replaced religion, its leaders considered spreading religious fanaticism beneficial to the world. As a result, people of that time left their homes to destroy each other. When a demon that causes destruction in the form of religion replaces something sacred like religion, people call it a deception. People are deeply afraid of deception. This is because deceptions have caused the world so much suffering.

We must study history with a sense of history. It is completely wrong to study history merely to remember events. History is created so that we can learn from past events and see when and how much religion has hurt us.

Let's not gloss over events, but try to understand them from a correct perspective. If religion hadn't existed at that time, and faith had been in its place, would this have happened? Certainly not.

Those who left their homes to kill each other were all hateful towards heretics. They presented a horrifying scene in which man had become the enemy of man, seeking each other for food. When man seeks man for food, understand that humanity has been lost, and savagery has taken over. Lacking food and transportation, they plundered and murdered Jews along the way, resulting in the deaths of many. Seeing this, the Eastern Emperor, upon reaching Constantine, had them cross the Bosphorus without waiting for another group. From there, when they entered the territory ruled by the Turks, they were killed.

The second group consisted of the armies of several influential feudal lords from Western Europe. In exchange for providing these armies with transportation and personal military support, the Eastern Emperor extracted a promise from them that the former territories of the empire, which had been seized by the Turks, would be returned to the Emperor upon their reconquest. Although this promise was not fully fulfilled and the Emperor's support was insufficient, the Crusader armies nevertheless achieved considerable success in this war.

Leaving Antioch in November 1098, the armies, having meted out punishment to the rulers of Tripolis, Tyre, and Caesarea along the way, reached Jerusalem in June 1099 and, after a five-week siege, captured it in July 1099. They brutally massacred the city's Muslim and Jewish inhabitants. Sectarianism reigned supreme here, and Muslim and Jewish children and women were mercilessly slaughtered.

The point here is not to see who won, but to see who lost, from a historical perspective. And if we consider this, humanity was certainly defeated. A large number of people lost their lives. Like vultures, people plundered each other's property, and even corpses were buried after checking to see if they were wearing any gold or silver jewelry. If so, they were removed, that is, looted. However, most corpses were left under the open sky for wild animals and birds.

Thus, in this war, despite being human, humanity had become demonic. Its demonic nature was rampant everywhere, and it reveled in slaughtering its own brothers. Christian and Islamic historians have attempted to establish this demonic nature as humanity, in favor of their respective religions. However, this is completely wrong. We must observe this war objectively and establish the fact that the naked dance that humanity was performing at that time was not a victory for humanity, but a defeat.

## Second Crusade (1147-1149)

When, in 1144, the Turkish ruler of Mosul, Imaduddin Zangi, seized Edessa from the Christian ruler, the Pope was requested for help, and on his orders, the famous monk Saint Bernard preached the Crusade. This preaching of war by a saint once again became a warning signal for humanity. It seemed that the clouds of destruction were gathering again. In reality, the sainthood of those who call themselves saints is not about promoting war, but about promoting peace. But when the so-called saints forget their religion, the demon of religion will surely perform its dance. Asking for help from the Pope meant that the Pope had a huge army of followers at his disposal. Acting on this request, the Pope commissioned one of his followers, Saint Bernard, to preach a crusade. The saint began spewing venom against those who opposed the faith, just as Peter had done during the first Crusade.

The Pope's involvement thus made it clear that the religious leaders at that time were also driven by self-interest. They saw the welfare of humanity only in how their own religion and position as gurus could be protected, and how they could be glorified and indirectly establish their rule over the world. It is also worth noting that Christian and Muslim historians have criticized the advice given by our sages and saints to kings, claiming that these people interfered in politics to establish their dominance. They have attempted to distort Indian history by calling this a Brahminical system. Yet, they have found no fault in the conduct of their so-called religious leaders, even today, despite the fact that their conduct has caused great harm to humanity. So be it.

Religious venom once again coursed through the people, and, reopening old wounds, everyone left their homes intent on killing one another. According to Wikipedia, for this war, two prominent Western European kings (Louis VII of France and Conrad III of Germany) marched by land through Constantinople with an army of 300,000 to Asia Minor. Their mutual hostility and the indifference of the Eastern Emperor thwarted their success. The German army was defeated at the Battle of Iconium in 1147, and the French at the Battle of Laodicea the following year. The defeated armies reached Jerusalem by sea via Antioch and, with the support of the king, laid siege to Damascus, but withdrew without capturing it. Thus, the war was a complete failure.

However, we believe that this war succeeded in spreading the poison of sectarianism that had begun with even greater intensity. From then until today, people have never considered how communal or religious thinking can be disruptive and frenzied. If we consider the mentality of the people of that time, we find that even though the war had failed, the war mentality was still showing no signs of abating. This is why people quickly prepared for the Third Crusade.

## Third Crusade (1188-1192)

When plunder, robbery, and rape become the primary objectives of governance, anarchy spreads everywhere. Anarchy is retaliated with anarchy, leading to widespread destruction. When the storm of conquests by religious rulers arose in the world, these storms too wreaked havoc everywhere.

Religious rulers, who based their rule on plunder, murder, robbery, and rape, forcibly established vast empires, but they were never successful in protecting these empires for long. The only reason for this was that by adopting the king's vices, his subjects also became imbued with similar virtues. When subjects become imbued with vices, they go beyond the king's control. A king is not created to inculcate vices in his subjects, but rather to foster virtues. For this, it is essential that the king himself possesses virtues.

From a religious perspective, the empires of these religious rulers, who sought to usurp other kingdoms and annex them, were often the cause of conflicts, strife, and the massacre of large numbers of people. Lasting peace never existed between them. Following this path, the Turkish rulers also succeeded in establishing a vast empire. The rise of Turkish power is believed to be the cause of this third war. Sultan Saladin (1137-1193), of the vast Turkish Empire, defeated and captured the Christian king of Jerusalem at the Battle of Hattin in 1187, establishing his control over Jerusalem.

After defending this port in 1188, the Christian army laid siege to another port, Acre, in August 1189 to capture it from Saladin. Saladin defeated the besiegers. When French forces arrived in April 1191 and English forces in June, Saladin withdrew his forces, leaving only the coastal portion of the Kingdom of Jerusalem, where these ports (Acre and Tyre) were located.

The three major European kings had made extensive preparations for this war, but their cooperation and mutual opposition led to failure. The first was the German Emperor Frederick the Red-faced (Barbarossa), who was over 80 years old. The second was the French King Philip Augustus, who led his army on ships from the port of Genoa, but after a year in Sicily due to a dispute with the King of England, he reached Acre in April 1181. The third, the leader of this Crusade, was King Richard I of England, who was also the Duke of a French territory and had been a close friend of the King of France during his father's reign. He gathered his army in France and accompanied the French army to the coast. The English fleet departed from there in 1189 and was present at the port of Marseille. This war, fought on communal lines, was also extremely destructive for humanity.

## The Fourth Crusade (1202-1204)

By now, the Pope's power had grown considerably. Just as the Caliph was the head of the religion among Muslims, the Pope held a similar position among Christians. The so-called religious leaders had mastered the art of conspiring to strengthen their power by inciting religious frenzy among the people. As a result, large populations of the world became followers of their respective abbots, subservient to their dictates. These religious leaders exploited these communal sentiments extensively. Consequently, even great emperors were forced to bow before them.

Pope Innocent III was the initiator of this war. He wanted the Christian world to put aside its differences, demonstrate unity, and succeed in driving the Muslims out of this holy land. He believed that the presence of Muslims had trampled this holy land, and Christians should listen to their silent voice. Therefore, he strived to establish unity among Christians. He was eager to work for the unity of Christians worldwide, so that the teachings of Jesus Christ could guide the world and be spread. The Pope's power was at its peak at this time. He could grant any kingdom to whomever he wished.

It is a well-known fact that whether it was the Caliph of Muslims or the Pope of Christians, they were not elected by the people; instead, they themselves created paths for themselves that ensured their lifetime appointment as Caliph or Pope. They then exploited the religious beliefs of the people, misleading and misguiding them, so that they could establish their dominance in the world and their power could not be challenged from anywhere. To fulfill this vested interest, they even attempted to turn the then monarchies, empires, and kings into puppets. Due to the rise and attachment of public sentiment to these religious leaders, kings were often forced to agree with them. Due to this, the common people felt as if the Caliph and the Pope were other forms of God on earth. If they did not accept what they said, they would surely go to hell.

In 1202, the Eastern Emperor Isaac II was blinded and deposed by his brother Alexius, who himself became emperor. Western armies arrived in Constantine by sea, defeated Alexius, and installed Isaac II on the throne. After his death, Constantine was again besieged, and after victory, Baldiwin, a feudal lord of Flanders (Belgium) in Western Europe, was crowned emperor. Thus, the Eastern Empire also came under the rule of the Western British, a position that lasted for 60 years.

In addition to this revolution, the British armies thoroughly looted the capital. They took wealth, gems, and artifacts from its treasury, and also plundered the famous Church of Saint Safia, whose roof is said to have been covered with 18 tons of gold by an emperor.

## The Children's Crusade

Since the rise of religious influence in world history, a new trend has emerged. Cruel rulers have committed inhumane atrocities against children and women. Such incidents were previously unheard of in human history. A particular look at India's Aryavarta period reveals not a single instance where any Indian ruler or head of a particular sect issued orders or carried out such atrocities against children and women.

A curious incident in world history occurred in 1212. A French farmer named Stephan, playing on the religious sentiments of the innocent public, declared that he had been sent by God to defeat the Muslims. He also declared that he would not rest until he had defeated them with his wisdom and strength. He claimed that this defeat of the Muslims would be at the hands of children. It was indeed this man's religious zeal that had a stunning impact on the public at the time. People were convinced by his words and believed that whatever he was saying was true.

This kind of religious zeal once again inflamed religious sentiments among the Christian population. For the first time in world history, 30,000 boys and girls under the age of 12 set sail from Marseille, the southern port of France, on seven ships for this mission. Blinded by religious faith, these children possessed an incredible faith, based on which they believed they would succeed in their mission. But this was not to be. Two ships sank with all their passengers, while the remaining passengers were enslaved and sold in Alexandria. Some of them were freed 17 years later through a treaty.

According to Wikipedia, in the same year, another zealot raised a second group of 20,000 children in Germany and led them to Geneva. The high priest there advised them to return. On their way back, many of them died on their journey through the mountains.

Children are a great asset to any country. This is why even the cruelest kings have considered it their duty to protect their nation's children. But what can the insane thinking of religion do to children? It's impossible to say. This horrific incident from history exemplifies this insane thinking: 50,000 children were made scapegoats by the insane thinking of religion.

Even after this, people haven't grown weary of the insane thinking of religion. Moreover, even today, people are seen forgetting these insane actions of religion and acting under its influence. This shows that human society doesn't want to learn anything from its past or its history. It believes in following the herd. Religion, too, is pleased with this herd mentality of people. He also does not want people to understand the truth of history, because if this happens then the ghost of religion will go away from people's minds.

## Fifth Crusade (1228-29)

In 1228-29, Emperor Frederick II entered into a treaty with the ruler of Egypt, acquiring the Holy Land's key sites: Jerusalem, Bethlehem, Nazareth, Taur, and Sidon, and their surrounding areas, and anointed himself King of Jerusalem.

## Sixth Crusade (1248-54)

A few years later, Jerusalem was again captured by Muslims. Jalaluddin, the Khwarezm Shah, ruler of Khoba, defeated by Genghis Khan, went west, and in 1144 captured Jerusalem, damaging its holy places and killing its inhabitants.

Following this, King Louis IX of France (who was canonized) attempted to retake these places twice between 1248 and 54. He sailed from France to Cyprus and from there captured Damietta in Myra in 1249. However, he was defeated in the Battle of Masor in 1250 and surrendered with his entire army. He recovered Damietta after paying a ransom of four hundred thousand gold coins. After this, he spent four years attempting to defend Acre, but was unsuccessful.

## Seventh Crusade (1270-72)

When the Turks captured Antioch from the Christians in 1268, Louis IX waged another Crusade. He hoped to convert the king of Tyre in North Africa to Christianity. Arriving there, he captured Carthage in 1270, but died of the plague within a short time. After his death, Prince Edward of England, later King Edward I, continued the war. Although he did not undertake any further operations in Africa, he reached Palestine via Sisila. He lifted the siege of Acre and forced the Muslims to sign a ten-year truce. Acre was the only place left in the hands of Christians in Palestine, and it was now the capital of their small kingdom. In 1291, the Turks captured it as well.

We have compiled this article with the help of Wikipedia. The sole purpose of this article is to show how many terrible wars the world has faced based on religion. And for how long political and religious power remained obsessed with religious fanaticism. That time was devoid of any consideration of moral or immoral, ethical or ethical immorality. Everything was under the influence of religious fanaticism.

Over time, when the powers of the Caliph and the Pope were either taken away or severely limited, the only reason was that after suffering so much plunder and violence, the people realized that it would be appropriate to free themselves from the contractors of religion. Although the interference of religious contractors in the lives of ordinary people persists even today, today's humanity should learn from the dark pages of history and, by implementing an education system that is consistent with the Vedas, ethics, religion, and the laws of nature, a global revolution should be organized to liberate the innocent public from the religious contractors. However, when the world is clearly divided into two camps, Christianity and Islam, the difficulties and impossibilities of such a global revolution can be easily understood.

All these wars tell us that humanity was slaughtered solely under the influence of communal sentiments. The world's two major religions, Christianity and Islam, were fighting for supremacy. They were not at all concerned about how much human blood had been shed or was being shed. Digging up the grave of history reveals how many people these two nations brought to the brink of destruction? How many did they murder to fill the grave of history with corpses? And how many people did they force to die prematurely? Will these sinners be punished for their sins on the Day of Judgment, or could there be a system in place even before that, where they would be made to pay the consequences of their sinful acts?

❐

*Chapter 10*

# Communalism in India: The British and the Congress

In ancient times, governance in India was based on a secular ideology. The primary objective was to ensure that every individual experienced freedom. The primary objective was to ensure that no one was bound or restricted, and that everyone could enjoy life safely. As long as this system functioned in India, peace prevailed in society.

Communalism and communal riots had no place in India's peace-loving society. If someone oppressed another, the rest of society would rise up in opposition to the oppressor. This forced anyone with a criminal mindset to think twice before committing a crime.

We have already clarified that the history of communalism, i.e., religious fanaticism and religious riots in India, begins with the invasion of Muslims. Every Islamic ruler in India encouraged such activities and, in the pursuit of religious service, attempted every possible atrocity.

When the British arrived in India, they saw that the Hindus of India neither accepted the atrocities of Muslims nor their communal views, nor did they like to sit with them due to their religious fanaticism. Their vision was to wage war against the infidels until the end of time. On the other hand, Hindu society, which strives to maintain its independence under all circumstances, believes in preserving its religious values, cultural identity, and the great traditions of its ancestors, which Islam seeks to eradicate. Islam has its own beliefs, while Hindus have their own, which prevent the two from coexisting. Muslims not only violate every single Hindu belief but also believe in the destruction of Hindus. This is why Hindus have never been able to accept Muslims as their own. Therefore, the Hindu community in the country remains suspicious of them.

## British Diplomacy

The British formed the impression about the country's Muslim community that they wanted to rule India for a long time based on religious fanaticism and to imbue it with their own image, that is, to transform it into a Darul Islam. The British carefully discerned that there were currently two heirs to the throne of India. One was a Hindu, who considered the country the sacred land of their ancestors and, on this basis, claimed their right to the throne. The other was a Muslim, who believed that their ancestors had conquered the land of India and that they alone had the right to the conquered. Understanding the mindset of both heirs, the British set out to advance their political interests. They not only exploited the political and social differences between the two from time to time, but also, where necessary, adopted communal policies to further their own interests. Where appropriate, they instigated conflict between the two, ensuring their victory, that is, gaining their own advantage.

The British cleverly rendered Muslims impotent in leadership. They made sure that no new Sultan would emerge, nor would any new Muslim kings be born to establish a new state. Few people notice that as soon as the British arrived in India and began their progress towards establishing their empire, new Muslim political leaders—Sultans and kings—stopped emerging.

To carry out this plan, the British began searching for people like Sir Syed Ahmed Khan from the very beginning. They continued this work over time, establishing them as leaders of Muslims. They began using them to promote bi-nationalism in the country. The British began promising Muslims the false promise of continuing to cooperate with them. If they ever had to leave India in the future, they would repay them for their loyalty, leaving them with a country of their own. To carry out this plan, the British provided Muslim communalism with their full cooperation and support from time to time. This allowed Muslim communalism to continue its rampant rampage in India even during the British era. This can be understood this way: whereas during the Mughal era, there were government-sponsored riots or religious fanaticism, now government-supported riots began to occur, indirectly supported by the British. Their sole objective was to keep Hindus under their control through Muslim communalism. Thus, the government's overall policy towards Hindus remained the same as during the Mughal era. Hindus continue to be victims of communal riots and violence. Even after understanding this truth, Congress leader Gandhiji did not consider the Mughal rule to be a period of subjugation for India.

## The British had explained to Muslims...

Muslim communalism in India had been state-sponsored. Recognizing this, the British offered their support to Muslims, subtly convincing them that they could continue their communal policies against Hindus. While offering their tacit support to Muslims, the British cautiously began referring to Muslim communalism as "communal riots." Even in these communal riots, it was often portrayed as if both Hindus and Muslims were at fault. In these riots, it was often portrayed as if Hindus were the culprits, even though Hindus were the most likely victims.

The Congress accepted India's Hindu-Muslim problem as defined and established by the way it was established. Because Congress was, in fact, the British's own brainchild. Even today, Congressmen continue to read the history that the British wrote about India as "*Brahma Vakya*." This is why, when Congress leader Sonia Gandhi considered introducing the Communal Violence Prevention Act, she believed that it was the majority community that perpetrated religious atrocities against the minority community. Therefore, Sonia Gandhi planned to suppress Hindu society through this law.

This tactic, or rather, this jargon, of the British, has led some to believe that communalism and riots in India only began during the British era. They believe that during the Mughal rule, peace prevailed throughout the country. There were no communal riots anywhere.

Thus, the British attempted to widen the already existing religious divide between Muslims and Hindus in India. This policy was crucial for the British to maintain their colonial system in India.

## Hindus Continued to Fight for Their Pride

The leaders of India's Hindu community had been unhappy with Muslim communalism from the very beginning, leading to periodic rebellions and revolutions. Unfortunately, when, under the leadership of Shivaji's successors, they succeeded in overthrowing Mughal rule in 1737, or even confining it to a small area, the British, who had come to India as traders, began to spread their political influence over India.

The Battle of Plassey in 1757 changed the course of the country's history. Hindu society had just been liberated from Mughal rule when the Battle of Plassey gradually paved the way for the British to establish themselves as a political power in India.

In 1857, when the British began preparations to organize centenary celebrations to celebrate their 100th year of rule in India, the country's Hindu power resolved not to allow such events. Keep in mind that the Hindu power of India was the same power which did not allow the Mughals and Turks to live in peace, then how could it allow the British to sit in peace?

## The British began to incite Muslim uprisings

The British succeeded in suppressing the 1857 revolution through a counter-revolution, but they subsequently began to fuel Muslim communalism in the country with even greater intensity. With their support, support, and encouragement, Sir Syed Ahmed Khan delivered an inflammatory speech in 1887 advocating two-nation theory in India, intensifying Muslim communalism.

Encouraging the riot-loving policies of Muslims, the British divided the country's major province, Bengal, in 1905 on communal grounds. They designated the Muslim-majority region as Muslim Bengal and the Hindu-majority region as Hindu Bengal. Although these were nominally known as East and West Bengal, the Hindu population of the country strongly opposed this, under the leadership of their revolutionary leaders, forcing the British government to yield.

It was no coincidence that Bengal was partitioned on communal lines in 1905, and the very next year, in 1906, Muslims were provided with a political platform to raise their voices, namely, the Muslim League. This political party was established by the British to fuel Muslim communalism. Its aim was to separate Muslims from Hindus and gradually prepare them for the demand for a new country.

By establishing the Muslim League, the British provided Muslims with a platform through which they could convey their views to the British. The British's approach to this Muslim platform was liberal and supportive from the very beginning. They had explained to its leaders even before its establishment that they would bring their demands to us through this platform and we would accept them with full government protection and support. This clearly demonstrates that the British's objective behind the establishment of the Muslim League was to fuel and amplify Muslim communalism and prepare for the disintegration of India.

Even if communal riots were necessary for this, a secret agreement was reached between the British and Muslims to instigate them under government protection. Had the Muslim League leaders been patriotic and their vision of living together with Hindus been true, they would not have formed the Muslim League with British patronage and support. Instead, they would have told the British:

"Our interests are completely safe in India, and we consider it our motherland. Therefore, do not use any deceit against us that would endanger the unity and integrity of our country."

But they did not do so. Moreover, when the National Assembly elections were held in 1945-46, 93% of the country's Muslims voted in support of the Muslim League, making it clear that they fully agreed with the Muslim League's demand for Pakistan.

The support given to the Muslim League's vision was silent. All Jinnahs were gone, who was with the country?

Thus, not only the Muslim leadership of that time, but also the Muslim voters and the general public supported the divisive policies of the Muslim League. This was because they considered Hindus to be their enemies and considered it inappropriate to live with them. Religion was deeply ingrained in their thinking. Driven by this very thinking, they harbored a riotous attitude towards Hindus and, whenever they had the opportunity, instigated riots against them.

## The British Implemented Their Thinking

Acting on the above-mentioned unwritten agreement between the British and Muslims, the British implemented the Morley-Minto Reforms of 1909 based on this policy. They later implemented the Government of India Act, and within it, they made every effort to encourage Muslim communalism. An examination of all these Acts and reform laws makes it clear that both Muslims and the British had jointly decided that Hindus were a race they both should rule over or oppress. Thus, the British colonial system in India transformed into a Hindu extermination system.

When the British announced the "Communal Award" in 1932, it began the game of Muslim appeasement in India. This was continued after the British left by their adopted son, Nehru, and his party, the Congress Party. Unfortunately, the Congress continues to pursue this policy of Muslim appeasement to this day. This rapidly initiated the process of communalization of Indian politics, which continues to this day.

Communalism also transformed a leader like Jinnah from being anti-Hindu to anti-national. Although he was born into a Hindu family, when he was influenced by Islamic communalism, he became not only anti-Hindu but also anti-national, demanding the disintegration of the country from the platform of his party, the Muslim League, at the Lahore session of 1940.

When Bengal Chief Minister Suhrawardy organized 'Direct Action Day' on August 16, 1946, and orchestrated the mass massacre of Hindus through communal riots, he not only had the support of the Muslim League but also the British. Moreover, even Congress leader Gandhi did not strongly disagree with him and, engaging in the despicable politics of Muslim appeasement, almost consented to this atrocity. Thus, by acting anti-Hindu, Congress proved itself to be anti-national. Because it is a universally accepted truth about this country that any person, ruler, or community that is anti-Hindu automatically becomes anti-national.

## Muslim Communalism after Independence

When India was divided in 1947, it was solely and solely due to Muslim communalism. However, historians and writers who harbored hatred for India committed the illogical and anti-national act of finding the seeds of Hindu communalism even in the conduct of revolutionary and Hindu leaders of that time who opposed Muslim communalism and their policy of inciting riots. They did so while agreeing with the British and Congress's thinking towards Muslim communalism. This same tendency can be seen even today among leftists and Congress members.

In their eyes, even opposing Muslim communalism is considered a sin, or rather, it is also termed as Hindu communalism. The reason is that even today, these people refer to Hindu organizations and parties as Hindu communal forces. Due to this mindset, they have deemed it necessary to teach and explain to students preparing for the IAS exam that various political parties in India adopt communalism to further their political interests.

This single sentence distorts reality. This double-faced statement makes the IAS student feel as if both Hindu and Muslim organizations are communal. The practical truth is that Hindu forces are actively working to control Islam's anti-national activities and communal thinking. Consider that Muslim communal forces, organizations, and terrorist groups are fulfilling the mission of Babur and Aurangzeb today. Whereas in today's times, Hindu organizations are playing the role of Maharana Pratap and Shivaji, who are fighting against the divisive forces of the country and are ensuring that this country is not divided again under any circumstances.

Just as great warriors of Hindu history like Maharana Pratap and Shivaji are viewed with disdain and hatred, the country's so-called secular parties and organizations view today's Hindu organizations and their leaders with the same attitude. In fact, just as politics has been criminalized instead of politicizing criminals, these pseudo-secular organizations and political parties have communalized politics instead of politicizing communalism.

## The Hypocrisy of India's Secular Parties

No secular leader in the country claims that Islamic fundamentalism is the sole cause of communalism and riots in India. Even Islamic scholars never appeal to their people to rise above the narrow-mindedness of Islamic fundamentalism, i.e., Darul Harb and Darul Islam, and to consider India as their own country and work for its progress. Turning a blind eye to this truth, all these political parties and so-called intellectuals of Islam attempt to mislead the people of the country, claiming that terrorism or Muslim communalism are resorted to by those who are victims of poverty, inequality, and illiteracy. The rest of the Muslim community has no connection to these issues.

If we consider these so-called causes of poverty, inequality, and illiteracy, it can be said that the Muslim community itself has created all three of these as a curse for itself. Because overpopulation breeds poverty, illiteracy, and inequality, a practice the Muslim community is engaged in. Furthermore, the people of Islam have considered it their privilege to avoid adopting modern education beyond religious education. When the Muslim community has resolved to neither pursue modern education, nor have fewer children, nor to align with the national mainstream, then who is responsible for creating inequality, poverty, and illiteracy in society? This is easily understood.

We believe that the government should make radical changes to the school curriculum. Today's students should be taught about the country's brave martyrs, revolutionaries, and historical figures who dedicated themselves to the nation and served under Islamic rule and later under British rule. The Congress mentality of establishing terrorists, traitors, and anti-national figures as historical figures must now be bid farewell. Decisions should be made to do what is right in the national interest, abandoning any policy of Muslim appeasement.

Islamic intellectuals should also take the initiative. They should enter the field with positive thinking and positive energy to ensure their contribution to nation-building. It has often been observed that some Muslims come forward to criticize Muslims, but they lack the support and protection they deserve from secular political parties, leaving them feeling vulnerable. In such a situation, it is also essential that such individuals receive full support from the government and social organizations. They should be encouraged to speak their good and true views openly. ❑

*Chapter 11*

# Muslim Communalism in the View of Scholars

## Anwar Shaikh says about Islam:

"Islamic culture is merely an extension of Arab imperialism. It has diluted the national identity of non-Arab Muslims to such an extent that they prefer to call themselves simply Muslims, rooted in Arab traditions, rather than Indians, Pakistanis, Iranians, or Afghans. Thus, they are easily provoked in the name of Islam, willing to do things they would not normally do. Furthermore, it is the religious duty of every Muslim to rule over non-Muslims, which makes this culture extremely aggressive.

As an aggressive culture, Islam is anti-democratic. This is because in Islam, the authority of government belongs to Allah. Humanity must unquestioningly follow the rules made by Him and Muhammad, no matter how irrelevant or outdated they may be. Autocracy is always the basis of aggression."

Another distinctive feature of Islam is that it glorifies violence and approves the murder, plunder, and abduction of non-Muslim women to spread the name of Allah, who claims to be omnipotent. Yet, he depends on humans to sing his praises. He also calls himself the most merciful. Furthermore, he permits the most despicable atrocities against those who refuse to accept him as divine. Murder, rape, robbery, and kidnapping are the worst forms of moral misconduct. Yet, Allah recognizes these as noble deeds for the Mujahideen, who yoke non-Muslims to the yoke of Islam, that is, convert them to Islam. The average person is astonished by this kind of morality, invented to incite aggression. A Muslim calls it "*Jihad*," meaning holy war, no matter how virtuous the means and methods used. (*Islam, p. 57, 58*)

Where communalism takes hold, democracy dies. This is because communalism does not believe in rationality and equality for all communities, whereas democracy advocates rationality and equality for all communities. Where even heinous crimes like murder, robbery, dacoity, and rape are considered conclusive proof of a particular community's attainment of heaven, or a certificate of enjoying pleasures with houris after death, thinking about religion is like searching for meat in an eagle's nest. This is the problem with Islam: before death, its followers are shown visions of the afterlife. In these visions, the more they oppress non-Muslims, the more they gain the right to create a better afterlife or to indulge in pleasures with houris.

## Yogiraj Sri Aurobindo's opinion is...

Yogiraj Sri Aurobindo, expressing his views on Islam, said:

"You can live in harmony with a religion whose principle is tolerance, but how can you live in peace with a religion whose principle is, 'I will not tolerate you?' How can you establish unity with such people (Muslims)? Surely Hindu-Muslim unity cannot be established on the basis that Muslims continue to convert Hindus while Hindus do not convert any Muslims." (*Reference: From a conversation on 23/7/1923, A.V. Purani's Evening Talks Sri Aurobindo, page 241*)

Yogi Aurobindo's approach was very practical and comprehensive. He understood the fundamental principle of Islam: no matter how much this religion preaches peace, its reality is that it does not like to live with others. It does not believe in peaceful coexistence. On the contrary, while feigning peaceful coexistence, it seeks to gradually destroy the other by digging out its roots, and its ultimate goal is to establish its own dominance. Therefore, it is constantly engaged in the process of converting non-Muslims. In such a situation, if Hindu society turns a blind eye to this kind of policy of Islam, then understand that it is heading towards self-destruction. Islam implemented this policy in its practical life from day one. It followed the same policy during India's freedom movement. It neither wanted to sit with Hindu society nor did it ever try to do so. Its communalism remained intact. Gandhiji should have learned from this view of Arvindji. But it is sad to say that Gandhiji never understood this reality about Islam, nor did he try to understand it.

## Savarkar's Opinion

Vinayak Damodar Savarkar was well aware of the reality of Muslims. He was clear that even after independence, special caution must be exercised with the followers of this sect, as they have nothing to do with Indian nationalism. The reality is that Indian nationalism, from the perspective of Islamic fundamentalism, poses a major obstacle, preventing it from establishing India as an Islamic state. Thus, Islamic fundamentalism, which seeks either to convert India into a Muslim state or to create a separate country for itself, can never establish harmony with India's peaceful Hindu society. It believes in the policy of deceit while living together.

Vinayak Damodar Savarkar said in 1939:

"Parsis, Christians, etc., are not a problem for India. When we become independent, they can easily be included in the category of Hindu citizens. But the case of Muslims is different. Whenever England withdraws its power from India, the Muslims of the country may prove to be a threat to the Indian state. The policy of the Muslim world to harbor its fanatic plan of establishing a Muslim state in India continues even today." (*Presidential address to the Hindu Mahasabha on December 30, 1939*)

## Dr. Bhimrao Ambedkar

"The second defect of Islam is that it is a system of social self-government and is incompatible with local self-government. Because the loyalty of Muslims is not to the country in which they live, but to the religious faith of which they belong. It is extremely difficult for a Muslim to think otherwise. Wherever Islam rules, there is his own faith." In other words, Islam does not allow a true Muslim to consider India his motherland or Hindus his close relatives. This is likely why a great Indian, yet a true Muslim, like Maulana Muhammad preferred to be buried in Jerusalem rather than in India." (*Reference: 'Pakistan and the Partition of India,' page 337*)

Whatever Dr. Ambedkar has written about Islam is true. Any Muslim who was formerly a Hindu and has now become a Muslim—the moment he converts from Hindu to Muslim—immediately becomes an enemy of India. Until the day before yesterday, he had his own Hindu family, his own community, his devotion to his gods and goddesses, and his devotion to religious scriptures like the Vedas. But he breaks all these loyalties in one stroke and becomes attached to the Kaaba. Not only this, he breaks all his ties and becomes fanatic against his former relatives. If asked to kill his own people, he readily agrees to do so. Thus, hatred and violence spread in his mind, and he takes no time in expressing them brutally. In such circumstances, it is not appropriate to expect brotherhood from people who believe in Islam. We all know that Dr. Ambedkar was an important leader of the Indian freedom movement. He observed events closely and understood the events very deeply. He also thoroughly analyzed with his intellect which side was wrong and which was right. Therefore, his opinion cannot be easily ignored.

Swami Shraddhanand ji's '*Shuddhi Movement*' was receiving strong reactions from Muslims. A Muslim named Maulana Abdul Bari used to advocate for an end to cow slaughter in order to gain Hindu support for the Khilafat Movement. However, when Swami Shraddhanand left the Congress party, disillusioned with Gandhiji's duplicitous policies, and realized that saving Hindu society was his top priority, this same Maulana Abdul Bari began spewing venom against him. He declared, "We can live with snakes and scorpions, but our coexistence with those who abandon Islam or those who encourage them to do so is impossible."

When complaints about this Maulana's remarks reached Gandhiji, Gandhiji declared, "I consider Abdul Bari to be God's innocent child." Furthermore, Gandhiji continued to call Swami Shraddhanand and the Arya Samajists quarrelsome and even criticized Swami Dayanand, the founder of the Arya Samaj. This led to anger against Gandhiji among the Arya Samaj members. Swami Shraddhanand also made it clear that if Muslims abandoned the process of converting Hindus, he too would consider ending his '*Shuddhi Movement*.' Muslims neither accepted nor did they accept Swami Shraddhanand's proposal.

Then Swami Shraddhanand ji was murdered. Dr. B.R. Ambedkar, saddened by Gandhi's behavior, wrote:

"Gandhi never called Muslims to account for the grave atrocities committed against Hindus (in order to achieve Hindu-Muslim unity). Muslim leaders not only failed to declare these murderers guilty, but instead praised them as 'religious martyrs.' They campaigned for the government to show them mercy. For example, Lahore barrister Barkat Ali (the culprit of the murder of Nathuramal Sharma in September 1934), arguing Abdul Qayyum's appeal, stated that according to Quranic law, the murder was absolutely justified. Therefore, he could not be held guilty of murder. This attitude of the Muslims was understandable, but Mr. Gandhi's behavior was completely unintelligible. Mr. Gandhi never urged the Muslim leadership to condemn these murders, but instead remained a mute spectator. (*Muslim Political Thought and Aspirations, author Purushottam Yog*) (*Amar Swami Publications Division, Ghaziabad*)

This book reveals that when the Congress issued a statement on the Communal Award, saying, "We neither approve nor disapprove of the Communal Award," it implied that the Congress had accepted the Communal Award. The direct implication of this was that upon implementation, Muslims would benefit and Hindus would suffer.

Responding to this, Dr. Ambedkar said,

"It grants the Muslim minority the right to self-determination on the question of electorates in Hindu provinces, but does not grant the same right to the Hindu minority in Muslim provinces.

In Hindu provinces, the Muslim minority is allowed to choose the type of electorate of its choice and the Hindu majority is not allowed to have any say in it. However, in Muslim provinces, the Muslim majority is allowed to choose the type of electorate of its choice and the Hindu minority is not allowed to have any say in it. Thus, Muslims have been given both a legal majority and separate electorates in Muslim provinces. Thus, it can be said that the Communal Award imposes Muslim rule on the Hindu minority. Which they can neither change nor influence."

How shameful it is that even when the government was directly siding with Muslims and oppressing Hindus, the Congress was still accepting the communal arbitration. That means, it was again taking a 'loss-making deal'.

## What does Guru Nanak say?

Guru Nanak saw the reality of Islam with his own eyes. He saw how the followers of Islam were committing various atrocities against Hindus. Then he said:

"The Sayyids, Sheikhs, Mughals, Pathans, etc., had all become extremely cruel and were inflicting terrible torture on Hindus. They threw Hindus in front of carnivorous birds like vultures. Many (Hindus) were killed by nails being driven into their bodies. Many other Hindus were torn to death by dogs. Those who refused to convert to Islam were tortured in many other ways. Performing yagnas and havans was prohibited, and those who violated these orders were forced to apologize. Beautiful Hindu women were abducted and forcibly kept in Muslim homes. Judges, bribed, twisted truth into lies through their decisions." (*Pan-Islamism Rolling Back, by Nanak Prakash and Premnath Joshi, p. 80*)

From the time of Guru Nanak to Gandhi's, Muslims had remained unchanged. Their cruelty and ruthless persecution of non-Muslims remained the same. They had not shied away from their beliefs and religious teachings. Yet, Gandhiji continued to trust them. He was confident that Muslims would abandon their teachings and, after understanding the realities of the country, decide to side with non-Muslims. To this end, Gandhiji did not hesitate to criticize or condemn even his own patriotic followers.

## Raja Rammohan Roy's Opinion

Raja Rammohan Roy also presented his true understanding of Muslims to the public. He understood fully that no Muslim could behave contrary to the verses of the Quran that instruct every Muslim to behave against non-Muslims. He deeply understood this. I understood that when a Muslim acts according to these verses, he becomes violent towards non-Muslims. Thus, these verses of the Quran are the root of all controversy.

That is why Raja Rammohan Roy said about Islam:

"Muslims have committed extreme atrocities on Hindus, and especially on Brahmins, because they have remained steadfast in Hinduism and have not abandoned their religion despite untold atrocities and threats of death by Muslims. Muslims have believed that the verses of the Quran are God's command for them, and they have determined that it is God's command for them to torture and kill idolaters (Hindus). According to Muslims, 'Of all idolaters (Hindus), Brahmins are the lowest.' This is why Muslims have become fanatics and have spared no effort in killing non-Muslims (Hindus, Buddhists, Christians, etc.) in religious frenzy." (*Reference: Complete Works of Raja Rammohan Roy, pp. 726-727*)

## Swami Dayanand Ji's Opinion

Swami Dayanand Ji Maharaj was the first great man who seriously reflected on the reasons for the loss of our country's independence. He observed that while the hypocrisy and superstition prevalent in our society were a significant reason for the loss of our independence, the policies of Islam were also greatly responsible. He also realized that controversial verses from the Quran were the reason for repeated communal riots in the country, disrupting peace. Because of these verses, every person who professes Islam is engaged in the game of plunder in society and the world. If these verses were banned or if the followers of Islam voluntarily removed them from their scriptures, peace and order could be established in society. Swami Ji presented a very serious reflection on these verses in "*Satyarth Prakash*." He was the first person who pointed out the disturbances and communal riots taking place in the society due to these verses and exposed the way the followers of Islam were fooling the Hindus by declaring Islam as a 'religion of peace'.

While reviewing the verses of Quran (*8:39, 41, pp. 151-153*), Swami Dayanand wrote in '*Satyarth Prakash*':

"Who else would be a peace-breaker other than the God of Muslims who fights and fights against such injustice? Now see, it is not the work of robbers in this religion that looting the whole world and getting it looted for the sake of Allah and Rasul? And to become God's sharer in the looted goods is to become a robber and to be a partisan of such robbers, It is a matter of great surprise that from where did such a book, such a God and such a prophet come into the world with such a title and to cause suffering to the people by disturbing the peace?" (*page 573*)

## Swami Vivekananda's Declaration

Swami Vivekananda also understood the truth of Islam and saw that the Quran never encourages any Muslim to befriend or maintain brotherhood with a non-Muslim. Therefore, he says,

"The Muhammadan faith, i.e., Islam, allows its followers to kill all those who do not subscribe to their faith, i.e., non-Muslims. The Quran clearly states, 'Kill non-Muslims if they do not convert to Islam.' They should be burnt in fire and beheaded with the sword." (*Vivekananda Vangmaya, Vol. 2, p. 335*)

Attacking Islam's policy of the sword, Swami Vivekananda writes elsewhere, "In this matter (Islam), Muslims were unique. They took every step forward with the edge of the sword, that is, with the Quran in one hand and the sword in the other, '*Accept the Quran or die, there is no other option*'.

You know from history how astonishingly successful they were with this. For six hundred years, no one could stop them. (Swami ji means that by understanding the reality of Islam, Hindu society will also have to abandon its state of laziness and negligence). (*From a speech given in California on January 28, 1900, Vol. 2, pp. 69-70*)"

"In this matter (Islam), Muslims today are the most ruthless and sectarian. Their main principle is: '*God (Allah) is one and Muhammad is his prophet.*' Everything beyond this is not only evil but must be destroyed immediately. Every man and woman who accepts this principle Anyone who does not fully believe in this should be killed after a moment's warning. Everything that does not conform to this form of worship should be destroyed immediately, and every book that teaches anything other than this should be burned. For the past five hundred years, there has been continuous bloodshed throughout the world, from the Pacific to the Atlantic. This is Mohammedanism! Yet, among these Muslims, wherever there has been a philosopher, he has certainly condemned these atrocities." (*Reference: From a speech given in Pasadena on February 3, 1900, Volume 4: Page 126*)

"For hundreds of years, wave after wave of foreign invaders have poured into India, ravaging and destroying it. Swords flashed here, and the Indian sky resounded with the slogans *'Fight and conquer for Allah.'* But these floods gradually subsided on their own, without altering India's ideals." (*Volume 4: Page 159*)

"For Muslims, Jews and Christians are not objects of extreme hatred. In their eyes, they are at least men of faith. But this is not the case with Hindus. According to them, Hindus are idol worshippers and despicable "infidels." Therefore, they deserve brutal murder in this life, and eternal hell awaits them after death. If Muslim sultans showed any kindness to the spiritual leaders and priests of the infidels, it was to allow them to live quietly until their last breath. This too was sometimes considered a great kindness. If a Muslim sultan's religious zeal was unusual or excessive, a massive yagna (sacrifice) of the "infidels" would be immediately arranged." (*Volume 4: 446*)

"You know that Hinduism does not persecute anyone. This is a country where all sects can live in peace and harmony. Muslims brought with them oppression and genocide, but before their arrival, peace prevailed here." (*Volume 5: Page 190*)

"There may be a religion that teaches extremely horrific teachings. For example, the Muhammadan faith (Islam) allows Muslims to kill all those who do not follow it. It is clearly written in the Quran that- 'Kill the unbelievers (non-Muslims). If they do not become Muhammadans, that is, Muslims.' They should be thrown into fire and beheaded with the sword. Now, if we tell a Muslim that this is wrong, he will naturally immediately ask, 'How do you know this? How do you know this is wrong?' My holy book (*the Quran*) says that this is right." (*From a speech in London on November 17, 1899, from Practical Vedanta, Part 3*)

If Gandhiji was truly leading our freedom movement and was the only leader above whom no one stood, he should have read and understood the views of his predecessors and other contemporary leaders, social reformers, and thinkers who were providing us with very factual information about Islam. But Gandhiji was unwilling to do any of this. Perhaps this was the greatest misfortune of India at that time, which was continuously leading it towards the horror of partition...?

❒

*Chapter 12*

# Muslim Communalism and the Congress

The British began exploiting the anti-Hindu nature of Muslims from day one. Following this policy, they exploited their anti-India nature to their fullest advantage. They repeatedly incited communal riots against Hindus by providing government protection to Muslims. This instigated communal riots against Hindus, creating the impression among Hindus that both Muslim and British forces had united against them and that their survival would be in danger if they joined forces.

When the Jallianwala Bagh massacre occurred, the British further exploited Muslim communalism to their advantage, inciting communal riots. Expressing their full sympathy for Muslims, they attempted to make Hindus feel isolated on this front. This communal riot greatly boosted Muslim morale. Consequently, the Kohat communal riots of 1924 occurred, in which Hindus suffered heavy losses.

In June 1928, Sardar Bhagat Singh wrote an article in "*Kirti*" about the Kohat riots. In it, he wrote, "The condition of India is currently very pathetic. Followers of one religion are sworn enemies of those of another. Now, to belong to one religion is to be a staunch enemy of the other. If you still don't believe this, just look at the recent riots in Lahore. How Muslims have killed innocent Sikhs and Hindus, and how the Sikhs have spared no effort.

This massacre was not carried out because a particular person was guilty, but because a particular person was a Hindu, Sikh, or Muslim. Simply being a Sikh or a Hindu was enough for Muslims to kill a person, and similarly, being a Muslim was sufficient reason for taking his life."

Pakistan's founder, Muhammad Ali Jinnah, was well aware of how the British were using him for their own selfish ends, but he wanted to continue being used by the British to achieve his larger objective: Pakistan. Although his core character was Hindu, as he was born a Hindu child in a Hindu home, he was also aware of how Hindus had looked upon him with contempt after he converted from Hinduism to Islam and how they had strongly condemned his deplorable act. He wanted to avenge this behavior by dividing the country. It would have been better if Jinnah had broken free from this thinking and become a Hindu again.

## Independent India's First Riot

Jinnah orchestrated the partition of the country, and independent India's first riot also took place in Kashmir. To regain the Kashmir Jinnah had been deprived of, he enlisted the help of tribals and began sending his soldiers disguised as tribals into India. In reality, Jinnah had easily obtained Pakistan through the tactics and tricks of the British. Therefore, he thought that he would succeed in acquiring Kashmir with the same ease. Jinnah, Pakistan's first Governor-General, was faced with the example of the massacre of Hindus in Bengal by Suhrawardy during the Direct Action Day in 1946. Consequently, he initiated the massacre of Pandits in Kashmir through his army disguised as tribals.

His thinking was that just as the morale of senior Congress leaders was shattered by the Hindu massacre during Direct

Action Day on August 16, 1946, a similar situation would befall India's leadership, as power in India was then in the hands of the same Congressmen who had led the Congress party during Direct Action Day. Jinnah's prediction was not wrong to any extent. It was fortunate for India that Sardar Patel, the Home Minister and Deputy Prime Minister at the time, was the country's Home Minister, whose wisdom and patriotism thwarted Jinnah's plans.

## Pakistan launched its first attack on India

Pakistan began its attack on Kashmir on September 3, 1947. India's Prime Minister, Pandit Jawaharlal Nehru, failed to provide timely and adequate support to the then Maharaja of Kashmir, Hari Singh, leaving him helpless in the face of Pakistan's attack. The king wanted to protect his subjects, but was unable to devise a way to counter them. Understanding the Maharaja's mindset, the Hindu population of Kashmir began fleeing. In this Pakistan-sponsored communal riot or attack, Pakistan succeeded in seizing a large portion of Kashmir from India, which remains under Pakistani control to this day. We call this area Pakistan-occupied Kashmir.

Thus, independent India's first riot proved detrimental to India and beneficial to the enemy. However, the then leadership failed to recognize this national loss and did not attempt to learn any lessons from it. They continued to pursue their policy of Muslim appeasement. This foolishness of the then leadership of the country and the Congress party inspired communal elements in the country to incite even more communal riots. These were the same people who could not go to Pakistan but remained in India with a Pakistani mentality. Pakistan named this operation Operation Gulmarg. Had Sardar Patel not been alert to this Pakistani action in time, Operation Gulmarg could have led to the annexation of all of Kashmir.

## The Nizam of Hyderabad's Anti-India Thinking

At that time, the demand for another Pakistan was being raised within India, and the Nizam of Hyderabad was leading that demand. The anti-national germs within him were stirring just as they were in Jinnah's head. The Nizam of Hyderabad adopted an anti-India stance from the very beginning and was determined to establish a Pakistan within India. Many have illogically attempted to blame the Hindu mentality of people like Veer Savarkar for the creation of Pakistan. Such people also ignore the Muslim communalism of the Nizam of Hyderabad.

If Pakistan was created due to Hindu communalism, then which Hindu communalism was responsible for the Nizam of Hyderabad's insistence on a separate Pakistan within the country? This was a clear example of Muslim communalism. The Nizam of Hyderabad refused to join India. This was why he did not sign the Instrument of Accession prepared for joining India. The Hindu-majority population of Hyderabad wanted the state to merge with India.

Kasim Rizvi, playing with the patriotic sentiments of the Hindu population, instigated riots and began massacring Hindus, forcing them to flee. Just as Pakistan had sent its army to Kashmir with the help of tribals, Qasim Rizvi named his army Razakars.

The point is that whether it was Pakistan or the Muslim Nizam of Hyderabad, their thinking and methods were the same. Both had the same goal: the destruction of Hindus. The communal bug was gnawing at the back of both their minds. Inspired and encouraged by this, they began chronicling riots in various places at the dawn of independent India. Both wanted to gain significant benefits by pressuring the then Congress leadership.

## Sardar Patel's Strong Leadership

From the very first day, Sardar Patel kept a close eye on the Muslim communalism and anti-national activities of the Nizam of Hyderabad and Junagadh. With his political acumen and courageous style, he succeeded in integrating these two princely states into India. In reality, this success belonged not to the entire Congress party or the then Indian government, but to Sardar Patel alone. If then-Prime Minister Nehru had his way, he could have capitulated to these two princely states, and we would have seen the creation of not one but two more Pakistans within India.

The Punjabi princely states of Nizam of Hyderabad and Junagadh merged with India, but Sardar Patel passed away soon after. After his death on December 15, 1950, Muslim communalism began to rise again.

Just two and a half years ago, the same Muslim communalism that the Congress and its leaders were seen defending and were absolutely unwilling to accept as responsible for the partition of the country, has once again regained its old form. According to the 2008 riot report, 654 riots occurred in Madhya Pradesh, 613 in Uttar Pradesh, and 341 in Karnataka by that time. During Prime Minister Nehru's tenure, 243 riots occurred between 1950 and 1964. If a detailed report of these riots were compiled and published, it would constitute a volume.

After Pandit Jawaharlal Nehru, Shastri became the Prime Minister of the country, but his tenure was brief. After him, Pandit Nehru's daughter, Indira Gandhi, became the Prime Minister of the country. During her tenure, 337 riots occurred in 15 states of India, which was nearly 100 more than the number of riots that occurred during her own father's tenure. When Indira Gandhi was assassinated in 1984, Rajiv Gandhi, her son, succeeded her as Prime Minister. His tenure lasted only five years, but within those five years, the country witnessed and endured 291 communal riots across 16 states.

## Hindus Exodus from Kashmir

Around this time, under the pseudo-secular governments of the country, a large number of Hindus were forced to flee Kashmir. The entire state was transformed into a den of communal riots. This was a period in Kashmir when every Muslim was free to riot in almost every street and neighborhood, 24 hours a day.

In these government-sponsored riots, communalism and religious fanaticism played out openly, with no one to stop them. Under these circumstances, it became utterly impossible for Hindus to remain there. All secular politics watched silently, while Hindus were forced to flee from one of the states of independent India. Lame, lame, secular governments did not take the displacement of Hindus seriously. They kept announcing plans to build housing for them, but failed to provide them with the existing housing they had already built. Perhaps it is difficult to find such an example of the helplessness of any government in the modern world other than India.

In fact, this exodus of Hindus from Kashmir was due to government-sponsored communal riots. Religion was the driving force behind these government-sponsored riots, whose sole objective was to de-Hindus Kashmir and then declare it an independent Muslim state.

## Why do communal riots occur?

The only question now is: why do these communal riots continue to occur? If we consider this question, we find that the Congress party's policy of Muslim appeasement provided the desired fuel for these communal riots. Congress continued to use Muslims as a vote bank.

Congress never encouraged Muslims to live together with the country's Hindu community. Nor were they ever taught or explained that the country's welfare lay in the coexistence of both communities. On the contrary, Congress repeatedly attempted to portray Muslims as being responsible for the partition of the country, not Jinnah, but Hindu-oriented leaders. Congress, however, defended them at that time and is committed to their defense even now, in independent India. This thinking and Congress's approach inspired Muslims to maintain their 36-degree alliance with Hindus. Furthermore, due to their perceived indirect support from the government, they began inciting frequent communal riots against Hindus.

Had Congress been serious about communal riots and taken concrete steps to enact stringent laws to suppress them from the outset, the history of riots in the country would have been different. It is quite possible that communal riots would not have occurred in the country at all.

Regarding communal riots, we should also keep in mind that when the Congress party was in power in Maharashtra between 2004 and 2008, 681 communal riots occurred in those five years. This is likely a record for so many riots in a single state in independent India in such a short period of time, and this was possible only during Congress rule.

Nearly 900 people were killed in the communal riots that broke out in Mumbai in 1993. Subsequently, 250 people were killed in the terrorist attacks on March 12, 1993. It is also a harsh truth about those riots that underworld don Dawood Ibrahim orchestrated them.

## The Business of Corpses

After all, the business of counting corpses and using them to further one's own ends is an age-old practice of Islam, one that its followers embrace with great affection even today. Despite knowing everything, the country's political landscape remained silent, and the pseudo-secular political parties and their leaders turned a blind eye to the truth. Governments lacked the courage to take action against underworld don Dawood Ibrahim. This is why this individual was able to run a parallel government. Consequently, he began influencing the national media by infiltrating his own people into it.

He also succeeded in infiltrating the national film industry with his anti-Hindu mindset. He began a conspiracy to cast Muslim heroes alongside Hindu girls. So-called Muslim writers and actors who had infiltrated the media and the film industry began making every effort to insult Hindu deities and defame Hindu society.

Just as the Direct Action Day in August 1946 had put the Congress party under psychological pressure for the creation of Pakistan, the numerous riots that took place in the country have similarly put the Congress party, its leaders, and its state governments under pressure from figures like Dawood Ibrahim. Due to this pressure, Dawood Ibrahim began to carry out all these tasks with great ease. In essence, he began preparing for a new Pakistan. The corpses did their job. Congress and its leaders continued to search for Hindus and Muslims among these corpses. Their eyes did not try to see that in the form of these corpses, neither Hindus nor Muslims were falling, but rather, it was the blood of Mother India that was falling.

In reality, the Muslim League had initiated the riots to force Congress to surrender before it. Muslim leaders in independent India began to use this same thinking of the Muslim League as a weapon for themselves. Just as Congress had tried to hide this truth before independence, it continued to do so after independence as well. This led to the further escalation of Muslim communalism.

## Congress distorted the country's history

Congress distorted history and employed those skilled in this game to distort history. Due to which the glory of Hindu history was hidden from the eyes of the nation. People singing the praises of Babur and Akbar rapidly became widespread in the country. People like Babur and Akbar were made national heroes in history.

Even in the Ram Janmabhoomi case, governments failed to speak out in time. Consequently, the case languished in court for decades. As a result, some enthusiastic Hindu youth demolished the Babri Masjid. Such action while the case was pending in court was also inappropriate. Meanwhile, Muslim communalism escalated to such an extent that when some Ram devotees, Kar Sevaks, returned to Godhra by train after performing Kar Seva in Ayodhya, their entire train compartment was set on fire by Muslim mobs, burning everyone alive.

This incident, which occurred on February 27, 2002, was a very tragic event in the history of independent India. 59 people were killed in this incident. Pakistan was involved in carrying out this incident. Narendra Modi is still criticized for the subsequent reaction to Godhra, but no one realizes that if Muslim communalists hadn't set fire to the carriage carrying karsevaks, Godhra wouldn't have happened. It's utterly foolish to view events from a one-sided perspective. If we delve into the facts and uncover the truth behind the events, much becomes clearer. Future generations will benefit from the findings. People can understand who was truly at fault, and if that mistake hadn't been made, we could have avoided a major historical tragedy.

Nearly 2,000 people were killed in the violent incidents throughout Gujarat. Had our leaders taken an interest in resolving the Ram Janmabhoomi dispute from day one and had the courage to assert that only Hindus have a right to the Ram Janmabhoomi, history would have been different. When politics becomes silent at times, incidents of disrobing are inevitable.

❑❑❑